Great Yachts

Great Yachts

Philip McCutchan

Crown Publishers, Inc. New York

Designed by Andrew Shoolbred

First English edition published by
Weidenfeld and Nicolson, London, 1979

First published in the USA by
Crown Publishers Inc., New York

Printed in Great Britain

Library of Congress Cataloging in Publication Data
McCutchan, Philip, 1920–
    Great yachts.

    Includes index.
    1. Yachts and yachting—History.   2. Yacht
racing—History. I. Title.
GV812.M32 1979   797.1'4   79–15806
ISBN 0–517–53915–2

I dedicate this book with love and gratitude to my wife Elizabeth, who has been of so much help in reading and checking the typescript and proofs.

Contents

Introduction

Yachting today falls naturally into the two very different categories of cruising and racing, and it is a matter of temperament, very largely, which one chooses: either a man likes a challenge or he does not. While cruising means comfort, time for reflection and philosophizing, fresh mornings at sea and strange ports, racing carries all the opposite attractions: racers are built for lightness and speed, not comfort, they are tough to sail in, and the very speed itself is tiring as the body is constantly thrown about by the vagaries of wind and weather. In a sense, of course, racing and cruising are complementary: racing can teach the most efficient use of the gear and the most effective sailing methods (though racers sometimes overstrain their boats and subject them to unnecessary stresses); and very often the search for speed and high performance in racing yachts results in technical advances and design improvements in cruisers too.

The term 'yacht' is of Dutch origin, and the Dutch it was who introduced the sport into Britain at the time of the restoration of King Charles II to the throne. Charles can be considered the father of yachting; a sailor at heart, he had a tremendous interest in his navy, while his predilection for pleasure and frivolity directed him towards pleasure boats, and a yacht – or, to use the Dutch term 'jaght' – is by definition one built for pleasure. A 'jaghtschip' was originally a fast, light vessel of war, but in time this description came to be applied to any sailing vessel of a good turn of speed; when anglicized as 'yacht', though the term was first applied to vessels used for state and royal purposes, the meaning broadened to include any vessel whose purpose was neither war nor trade but purely pleasure.

OPPOSITE *Sunbeam*, the superbly elegant three-masted topsail schooner built for Sir Thomas Brassey in 1874. He sailed her round the world two years later, a trip which took 425 days, and he was the first man to make the voyage.

The steam yachts of the very rich in the days before the First World War were something not far short of fantasy. The life aboard was one of freedom and indulgence, in which expense was never even considered. Often they provided a setting for over-eating, over-drinking, and adultery – and for both the initiation and the demise of marriages. Starry nights at sea can be a powerful romantic influence on men and women alike; at sea there is an automatic cut-off from the shore and all its restrictions, and inhibitions tend to be blown along the four winds. The great private yachts were worlds in miniature, like the ocean liners themselves that once sailed from Tilbury to Sydney and Bombay, from Liverpool to Canada and South America, from Southampton to New York and the Cape, with the difference that the yachts could follow whatever course their owner chose to set.

No detail was overlooked in providing comfortable interiors to these seaborne palaces; the scale was lavish in the extreme, and nowhere more so than in the great British royal yachts named in succession *Victoria and Albert*. Aboard the old *V and A* – as each became affectionately known to a loyal public – the list of stores was said to itemize 'pot, chamber, with two gold bands and crown, for use of H.M. The King; pot, chamber, with one gold band and crown, for use of H.M. The Queen.' Women's lib had not yet arrived to bring equality to the royal bedroom.

Until the start of the Second World War wealth was essential for the owners of racers as well as steam-yacht cruisers. Though not all were famous, rich they had to be on a scale that is no longer possible or relevant today. Many were characters, one of the most famous being Sir Thomas Lipton. A personal friend of King Edward VII (known as Old Tum-Tum), he challenged for the America's Cup with his *Shamrocks* no less than three times during Edward VII's lifetime though even his royal friend, then Prince of Wales, had had to cut down on the grounds of expense.

Some of the paid crews were as well known as the owners for their eccentricity: a member of the noted yacht-skippering family of Parker of Southampton, when asked, peevishly, by King George V why the weather was so bad during a certain Cowes Week, blamed it fair and square on the Labour Government.

Fine seamanship was shown by the great racing yachtsmen of these earlier days, and as time went by it was they alone who carried on the traditions of the iron men who had driven the great windjammers and clippers around Cape Horn to South American and Australian ports, or brought the season's tea racing home from China by way of the Sunda Strait. As commercial sail began to leave the seas and the great merchant ports of Britain, America, the Continent and Australia resembled less and less a 'forest of masts and yards', the sail borne by the ocean and coastal yachtsmen became a constant and welcome reminder of a great race of men.

1 Early Yachts

*T*he *Surprise*, first in a long line of royal yachts, was far from glamorous; she was an ordinary coal-brig in which, after the battle of Worcester in August 1651, Charles II completed his escape to France with the help of his friends and the brig's master, Captain Nicholas Tattersall.

Having fled to the Sussex coast, pursued by the victorious armies of Oliver Cromwell, the King rested at the tiny village of Brighthelmstone – later to become Brighton – where he met Captain Tattersall who, for a cash-down sum of £60, agreed to embark the royal party. Tattersall was then kept all night at the George Inn, smoking and drinking with the King and his companions. This was in case he should be prevented at the last moment by his wife from assisting the King – as had happened at Charmouth during earlier negotiations.

However, two hours after midnight all was well: with Tattersall present, the King rode a little way west to the creek at Shoreham, whence Tattersall had earlier brought the *Surprise* from Shoreham harbour; and between 7 and 8 a.m. on Wednesday 15 October, Tattersall sailed, ostensibly along the coast for Poole in Dorset. At 5 p.m. that evening he altered course towards the coast of France, noting that His Majesty had a good knowledge of navigation and was keeping himself occupied on deck by directing the coal-brig's course. The French coast was sighted next morning, but the tide failed them and the wind shifted suddenly; *Surprise* was forced to anchor two miles off Fécamp, due south of Brighthelmstone, and the King, with his companion Lord Wilmot, was rowed ashore in the cockboat. Soon after they had landed in safety the wind shifted again and Tattersall sailed for Poole, no one suspecting that he had already visited France and safely landed his royal passenger.

At the Restoration Tattersall enlarged and embellished the *Surprise*, and moored her in the Thames opposite Whitehall as a reminder to His Majesty of his valuable services. These were indeed recognized and he was rewarded with a pension of £100 a year, to be paid to his wife Susan after his death, and then to his son Nicholas or his daughter, also named Susan. The last recipient of this long-lasting pension was Sir John Bridger, a great-grandson of Tattersall.

Shortly after the *Surprise* had been so strategically placed for the King's

ABOVE The *Royal Caroline*. Originally owned by George I and known as *Peregrine*, she was rebuilt and renamed in the reign of George II.

RIGHT George III's *Royal Sovereign*, launched at Deptford in 1804. Ship-rigged and armed, she was one of the largest royal yachts of her time.

attention, she was entered into the Royal Navy and her name altered to *Royal Escape*, with Tattersall in command, though he had arranged for a reversion of his Captain's pay in favour of his son Nicholas. In the Navy List of 1684 the *Royal Escape* is described as a small vessel of 34 tons, ten men, and no guns; at the time of the King's voyage in her she carried a crew of only four men and a boy, in addition to her master. After the King's death in 1685 she was sadly neglected; and she ended her life in one of the Deptford dockyards in a gradually worsening state of decay and dereliction; finally, more than a hundred years later – which speaks well enough for the stout timbers of the day – she was broken up to provide fuel.

During the reign of Charles II there were no less than 27 royal pleasure yachts all told, among them the *Mary*, given to the King by the Dutch in 1660. Of 100 tons and thus on the large side for those days, she was wrecked on the Skerries 15 years later. Charles owned a number of other yachts of varying tonnages, mostly smaller than the *Mary*.

Under the aegis of William of Orange eight royal yachts were built, some of them manned by up to 250 men, while Queen Anne's reign produced *Charlot* of 155 tons, re-rigged as a ketch in 1761 and named *Augusta*. Under the Hanoverian kings the use of royal yachts was continued, George I having 15 built at different stages of his reign. On his accession in 1714 he had crossed from the Continent aboard the 14-year-old *Peregrine*, renamed *Carolina* in 1716; rebuilt in the reign of George II she became the *Royal Caroline*, but in 1749 was returned to the Navy under her old name of *Peregrine*. George II made good use of his *William and Mary*, and also sailed eight other yachts of varying rigs and tonnages. George III built another *Augusta* in 1771 and followed her up with *Dublin* of 148 tons, *Portsmouth* of 68 tons, and *Bolton* of 42 tons. But outstanding was the *Royal Sovereign*, launched from Deptford in 1804. She was ship-rigged, copper-sheathed, and carried eight guns. Richly ornamented with leaves and medallions and a great deal of gingerbread work, her figurehead was of the King himself wearing his imperial crown, while Neptune, lording it aft, brandished his trident.

A long time before Charles II popularized yachting, some private vessels had in fact been built purely for pleasure purposes; but it was not until the Dutch introduced a habitable design and a suitable rig, derived from the *jaghtschips* (fast despatch vessels), that the business of pleasure sailing got fully under way. In the seventeenth century the Dutch developed their sloop-rigged pleasure vessels, and it was they who first used the gaff – a spar for extending the top of a fore-and-aft sail – and the leeboard (of assistance in sailing close-hauled); however, the leeboard was soon to be replaced by the straight keel which in the case of deeper draught vessels was used to prevent falling off the wind. Other modifications from the Dutch design were introduced to cope with English Channel conditions. In America, to which country the Dutch also exported the concept of the leeboard, development took the form of the centreboard drop keel. In the 1660s an early catamaran was developed as a breakaway from the Dutch tradition by Sir William Petty, a statistician and economist who was believed to have obtained his nautical ideas from seamen who had observed such craft in India.

Perhaps the first ocean racing to be seen off the British coasts was when Petty's catamaran *The Experiment* won its owner £50 by beating the packet-boat from Holyhead to Dublin in July 1663. *The Experiment* reached Dublin at 5 p.m., 15 hours before the packet-boat: such was the surprise when the catamaran came in that it was assumed the packet-boat had gone down. Later *The Experiment* featured in another and more official race – against the King's barge and a boat from a man-o'-war. Despite the loss of a rudder, Petty's weird craft was the winner. However, catamarans received a setback when one of Petty's double-hull vessels, *en route* for the West Indies, went down in the Bay of Biscay; and it was very many years before the concept was to be revived.

The eighteenth century saw the rise of the great yacht clubs in Britain, the first (in 1720) being the Royal Cork Yacht Club, first known as the Water Club of Cork. This was situated on Haulbowline Island where, until the Irish Free State came into being in 1922, the British Army and Navy maintained a fortified base. The club was chiefly social and indulged more in resplendent regattas than in competitive racing; it has the distinction of being the most senior of them all. In its early days formality and strict etiquette were the rule. The annual procession of boats to sea under their Admiral resembled the setting forth of a fleet of the King's ships of war, the annually-elected Admiral wearing his flag proudly and leading his squadrons forth with beating drums and sounding trumpets to receive due honour and acclaim. Indeed, all the proceedings were conducted along Royal Naval lines, and the club rules read rather like King's Regulations and Admiralty Instructions for the Navy, if not the Articles of War themselves – which threatened death for all manner of nautical crimes. Formation sailing was practised and the vessels moved to the sound of gunfire signals, of which there were always an inordinate number; forfeits were introduced when, on club-day rendezvous, those boats that were not in sight as the Admiral came abeam of the castle were fined a half-crown to be put towards the gunpowder fund. Dress was strictly ordered: no long-tailed wigs, no voluminous sleeves, no ruffles; while on another tack, even the Admiral was not permitted to bring aboard more than two dozen bottles of wine.

The next club to be founded was the Cumberland Sailing Society, better known as the Cumberland Fleet, in 1775. It was named after the Duke of Cumberland, George III's brother, who had begun to encourage the sport in a big way. The club, based on the Thames, was later to become the Royal Thames Yacht Club. It boasted a very wide membership from its inception, a membership drawn from all classes – gentry, professional men, merchants, men-about-town – the only persons barred being those who earned their living from the hiring-out of pleasure craft. In its first year the Duke of Cumberland presented a silver cup to the club, to be competed for in a race from Westminster Bridge to Putney Bridge and back, the event being open to boats between two and five tons burden.

This race was held on 13 July and there were 20 entries. The Duke of

OPPOSITE, ABOVE Cork Harbour: the River Lee, home of the Water Club of Cork, first of the great yacht clubs and later to become the Royal Cork Yacht Club.

OPPOSITE, BELOW The Caernarvon Regatta of 1849.

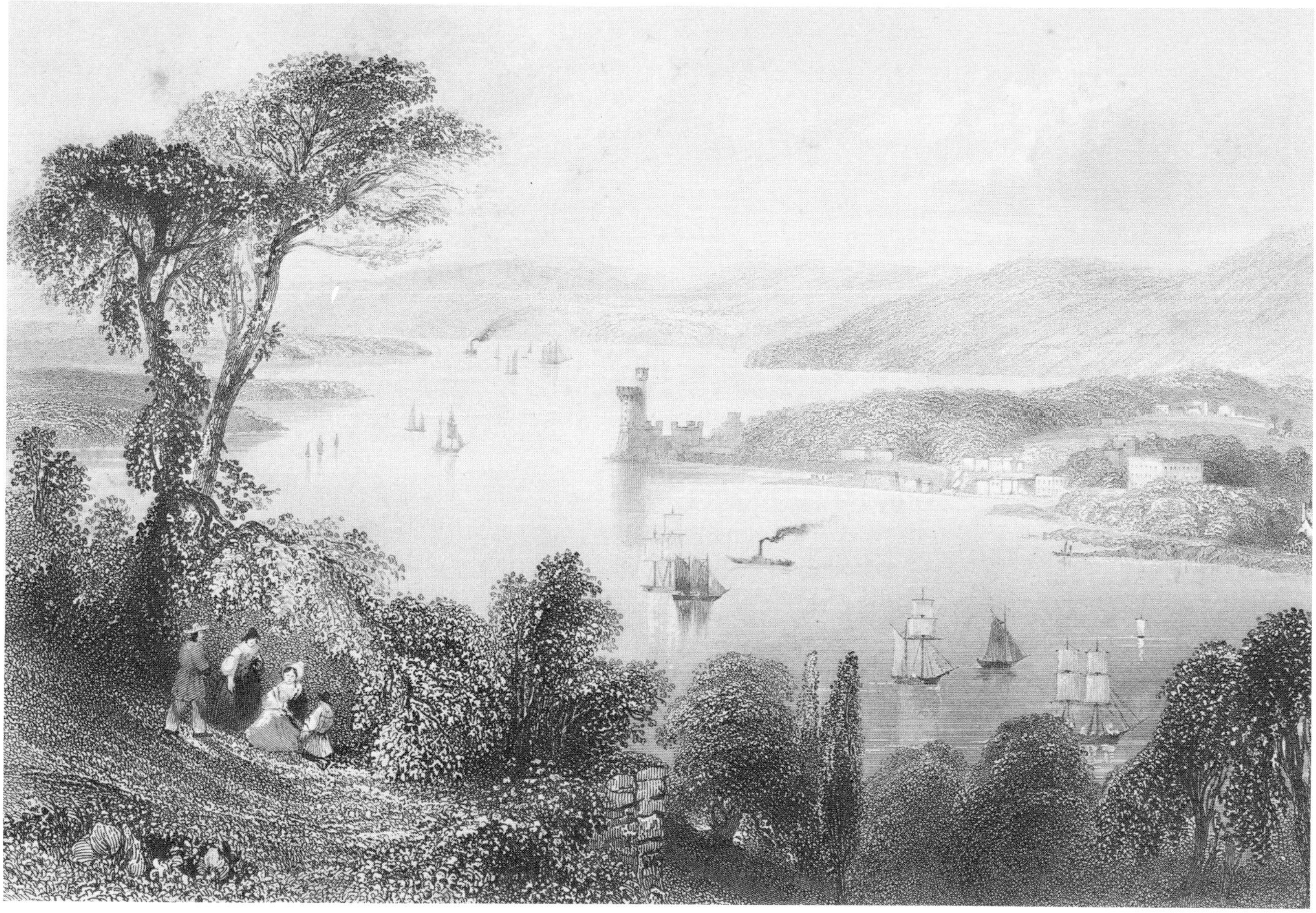

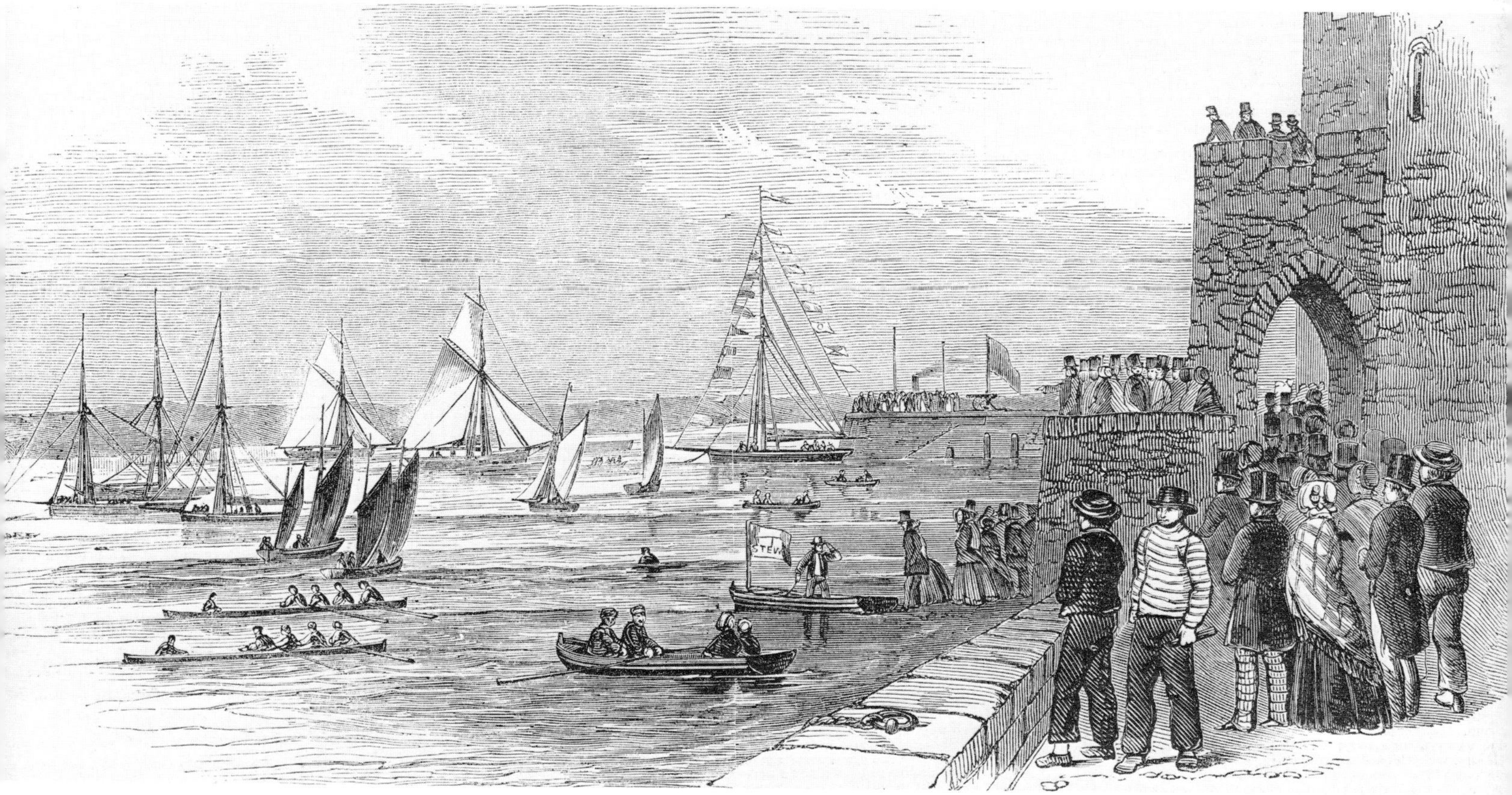

Cumberland attended in his state barge with the Royal Standard hoisted, accompanied by another vessel with a band embarked. The winner was *Aurora*, a yacht owned by a Mr Perkins of Ludgate Hill. After the finish, toasts were drunk with full ceremony in claret, which was handed round in the winner's cup by a butler, to the accompaniment of vociferous cheering from the thousands of spectators, the blaring of brass bands, and many salvoes of artillery. After such splendour, it is sad to record that it was as the result of a dispute among members of the Cumberland Fleet that the Thames Yacht Club, not yet Royal, was formed; it was in fact a breakaway group. In 1823 the Cumberland Fleet changed its name to His Majesty's Coronation Sailing Society, and two captains, as the owners were referred to, disputed the interpretation of the somewhat embryonic rules; supporters of one of the parties then resigned in a body to found the Thames Yacht Club.

The first event of the new club took place in September 1823: Blackfriars Bridge to Cumberland Gardens for a cup valued at 25 guineas. After this, two races took place every year until 1840. In the meantime the Duke of Clarence, later William IV, the Sailor King, had become the club's patron and his appointment led to further races; when the Duke succeeded to the throne in 1830 the club was honoured by the addition of Royal to its title. In 1848 the club was awarded, by Admiralty warrant, the right to wear the Blue Ensign. In May 1866 the Nore to Dover Race was instituted and in 1874 the Prince of Wales, later Edward VII, became Commodore; Thomas Brassey of *Sunbeam* fame, later Lord Brassey, joined the King as Rear-Commodore. On the occasion of the Queen's Golden Jubilee in 1887, the Royal Thames gave a prize of 1,000 guineas for a Round Britain sailing race, Dover being the finish line.

These events were not in fact the first races to receive royal patronage, for back in 1749 George III, then Prince of Wales, had become patron and trophy-presenter of the first of all races for a cup. Held in August, this was from Greenwich to the Nore and back, and the cup was won by the *Princess Augusta*, owned by a Mr George Bellas. The *Gentleman's Magazine* of the day says: 'His Royal Highness the Prince of Wales, with five or six attendants in his Chinese Barge and the rowers in Chinese habits, drove gently before for some time and a crowd of boats about him, the people frequently huzzaing, at which he pulled off his hat.'

The Royal Yacht Squadron

In 1815 the Yacht Club was formed, to become the Royal Yacht Squadron in 1833, with the right – granted in 1829 – to wear the White Ensign. Its members, exclusively of the aristocracy and gentry, wore a uniform of a blue jacket, single-breasted and short in the body, with white trousers; it was not unlike the uniform worn by petty officers in the Navy of the day, whose short jackets were possibly the forerunners of the 'bum-freezer' worn more recently as mess dress by naval officers. These were the days of full-blooded, hard-drinking men, whose roistering and uninhibited ways included a vigorous retaliation in the face of misfortune. In 1829, for instance, a race took place between *Menai*, *Lulworth* and *Louisa*, the

ABOVE Edward VII, when Prince of Wales, starting the celebratory race in the Queen's Diamond Jubilee Year.

RIGHT *Genesta* and *Irex* competing in the Jubilee race.

BELOW William IV of England, known as the 'Sailor King' on account of his interest in the Navy and the sea.

first two owned by untitled gentlemen, the third by Lord Belfast. *Menai* had gone hard aground after rounding the Nab shoal when *Lulworth* and *Louisa* collided, just as they were nearing Cowes at the finish. In true Royal Naval fashion, Belfast's men, encouraged by many warlike shouts, drew cutlasses and entered battle, slicing through the enemy's boom lacing as well as her reef pendant. Not to be outdone, *Lulworth*'s bold sailors hacked back. The official decision was reached that to cut away rigging with axes was not justified, whereupon Lord Belfast announced that in future he would cut in half any vessel attempting to cross his bows when tacking.

Lord Belfast was not, of course, renowned only for his arrogance and cutlass drill: it was he who built the famous *Waterwitch*, brig-rigged (two masts, square sail on both) and one of the fastest sailers of her day – soon to be copied by the Admiralty for naval use.

Some of the vessels owned by members of the Royal Yacht Squadron were quite remarkably warlike. Lord Cardigan of Light Brigade fame took his yacht to the Crimea, wearing full uniform with spurs when aboard. Lord Yarborough, Commodore in 1835, owned the 351-ton yacht *Falcon*, which was ship-rigged (square sail on all three masts) and equipped with a broadside of 11 cannon. The Duke of Portland's 350-ton brig *Pantaloon*, built in the Duke's own yard at Troon in Ayrshire, was commanded by a sailing master who, in his RN days, had been a member of one of the Navy's press gangs: any stray men below the estate of gentleman they happened to catch were rounded up for immediate sea service.

In 1838 the Royal London Yacht Club, first known as the Arundel Yacht Club, was founded, and then thick and fast came the Royal Western at Plymouth, the Royal Northern on the Clyde, the Royal Anglesey at Beaumaris, the Royal Southern at Hamble near Southampton (where now is kept *Britannia*'s racing flag presented by Edward VIII and Queen Mary in 1936), and very many more. The British Empire responded with the Gibraltar Yacht Club, later Royal, while in the farther dominions and colonies other great clubs were formed: in 1838 the Royal Hobart Regatta Association was born, in 1844 the Royal Bermuda Yacht Club, in 1867 the Royal Prince Alfred Yacht Club of Sydney, in 1869 the Royal South Australian Yacht Squadron at Adelaide and in 1875 the Royal Perth Yacht Club of Western Australia. In later years many others were to follow, indicating the growing nation-wide – indeed world-wide – popularity of the sport and the social occasions that went with it; but the Royal Yacht Squadron remained the pinnacle, guarding its membership list jealously, resisting for as long as possible the intrusion of trade and industry – as was witnessed by the long exclusion of Sir Thomas Lipton. When Victoria celebrated her Golden Jubilee in 1887, the RYS marked the occasion by a great race from Cowes to Cherbourg via the Nab Lightship and back to Cowes by the Eddystone Lighthouse, the homeward course being south of the Isle of Wight and the Nab. The race was for schooners, cutters and yawls above 30 tons, British and foreign, though in fact there were no foreign entries, and the prize of £500 was won by John Mulholland's schooner *Egeria*.

ABOVE West Cowes in 1823, from an engraving by William Daniell.

RIGHT The ship-rigged *Falcon* carrying 11 cannon, 351 tons. *Falcon* was owned by Lord Yarborough, Commodore of the Royal Yacht Squadron in 1835.

A wise and wealthy man once remarked that if a man needed to ask what it cost to run a yacht, then he couldn't afford to run it. Yachting was a rich man's pastime – the names of those who indulged in the nineteenth and early twentieth centuries were enough indication of this: the Dukes of Portland, Norfolk and Leeds, Lord Vernon, Sir Richard Williams-Bulkeley, Lord Iveagh of the Guinness family, Lord Francis Cecil, the Earl of Caledon, the Marquis of Ailsa and many others. Here were no Chichesters, no Chay Blyths. There was no sponsorship and the expenses were enormous, constant repair bills having to be met with a smile, bills that were infinitely larger in real money terms than today's because the vessels themselves were much larger, many of them carrying three masts with a huge sail area, comparable with that of a man-o'-war or a merchantman. The crews were large, so, therefore, was the wages bill: 30 in a racing crew was not unusual. The deck gear was vast compared with today's racers: spars, sails, blocks and rope by the hundreds of fathoms. But if the lavishness made possible by wealth had remained constant, rigs and types of vessels were always changing: the day of the schooner rig was already passing, to be replaced by the gaff-rigged cutter. Perhaps the epitome of schooner-rigged vessels was the famous *America*, whose first arrival in Cowes in 1851 altered the future course of yachting. The Queen's Cup had just been thrown into the ring, as it were, and was available by courtesy of the Royal Yacht Squadron to the world. Under Captain John Stevens, the 170-ton *America* of New York was the first of her nationality to come to Britain.

After a dispute over time allowances, *America*'s owner withdrew from the race for the Queen's Cup, and it was held without her. But the Royal Yacht Squadron decided, in the interests of fair play, to offer another cup for a race around the Isle of Wight; in this *America* took part, Queen Victoria and Prince Albert watching from the *Victoria and Albert*, the royal yacht of the day. It is a matter of history that *America* outraced all her rivals, coming home almost 20 minutes ahead of her next astern, the 47-ton cutter *Aurora*. The cup was hers – henceforth known as the America's Cup, not the Queen's, being hers alone by right of conquest.

Early days in America

The first recorded American pleasure boat or yacht was John C. Stevens' 20-ft *Diver*, built in 1809, followed in 1816, the year after Waterloo, by *Trouble*. Fifty-six feet in length and carrying two masts, *Trouble* was a good seaboat and a comfortable one; success with her encouraged Stevens to build more and more experimental prototypes, some of which were failures, some being subsequently handed over to the United States Government for use in the coastguard service. In 1835 came the first organized race, in which John P. Cushing's schooner *Sylph* raced Stevens' *Wave* off Cape Cod. By 1844 the numbers of yacht owners had grown to such proportions that a meeting held aboard Stevens' yacht *Gimcrack* led to the formation of the New York Yacht Club with Stevens himself as its first Commodore. Five years later the Southern Yacht Club was founded. From then on the sport grew rapidly, and some large yachts began

LEFT The trophy for the America's Cup race, first won by the US cutter *America* in 1851. Despite numerous challenges from Britain, and more recently from Australia, the cup has remained in the United States ever since.

RIGHT John C. Stevens (1785–1857), first Commodore of the New York Yacht Club and part owner of the great *America*.

BELOW Spectators at the New York Yacht Club's Annual Regatta, 10 June 1869.

to come along, notably Stevens' 160-ton sloop *Maria*, built by William Capes of Hoboken, and the schooners *La Coquille*, *Brenda* and *Cygnet*. *Maria* was a first-class racer, winning many trophies. Of 111 ft in length, she had a 26-ft 6-in beam, 5,790 sq ft of canvas and two centreboards, the after one being used to assist the steering. In 1849 *Brenda* raced against the British-owned *Pearl* and beat her – in the first recorded international race – by a margin of only 55 seconds.

America was jointly owned by Stevens and a number of associates, including his brother E. A. Stevens, and built by George Steers and W. H. Brown. She was intended to be a crack boat and much money was lavished on her. After her victory over Britain in the Royal Yacht Squadron's cup, she had an enormous influence on American yacht design, with everyone trying to re-design their boats along her lines. However, at the close of the 1851 racing season, she was transferred to the ownership of Lord de Blaquiere; she went to Britain, where she remained for some ten years; then, back in America during the Civil War, she sailed the seas in the interests of the Southern Confederate States. Sunk in Florida, she was raised to take part in the blockade of Charleston, and she later became a midshipman's training ship at the Naval Academy at Annapolis in Maryland. But, a racer to the end, she made a come-back in 1870 when she was refitted at staggering cost to race against the British *Cambria* for the America's Cup, her own cup, under the ownership of the United States Government itself. In the event she in fact took fourth place but came in ahead of the British entry. After many vicissitudes, the old *America* was bought by a yacht club in the eastern states for use as a floating clubhouse. Finally, in 1924, she was returned to Annapolis to become a nautical museum.

The racing yachts of the late nineteenth century were in many cases – perhaps most – not just racers: much 'gracious living' went on aboard them, and in the fine, spacious saloons, kings, presidents and the very rich were entertained to superb food and drink. Such a yacht was *Galatea*, a large-class cutter owned by a retired British naval officer, William Henn, which made an unsuccessful challenge for the America's Cup in 1886. Her saloon was fabulous and, by today's frugal standards, incredible: tiger skins lay atop expensive carpeting, cushioned sofas and rich door hangings abounded, the walls were adorned with valuable pictures, just like any wealthy Englishman's home ashore, and an exotic variety of plants stood in front of an ornate fireplace. In its time, none of this seemed incongruous – even on a racing yacht.

2 State Splendour and Rivalry

*T*he British royal yacht in use when Queen Victoria came to the throne in 1837 was the three-masted man-o'-war *Royal George*, next of her name after the more famous battleship in which Rear-Admiral Kempenfelt had perished with all his ship's company when she capsized in Portsmouth Dockyard on 29 August 1782. The royal yacht served four monarchs: George III, George IV, William IV and Victoria.

The Queen was an indefatigable traveller, especially on the railways, which she much enjoyed; the sea did not appeal to her so much and she was an indifferent sailor, while her husband Prince Albert was a worse one, growing pale and queasy the moment he spied a ship. In Victoria's early days, before she came to the throne, the royal yachts included the sailing vessel *Emerald*; during a voyage to Plymouth as a girl Victoria was sick for half an hour, but later managed to eat a hot mutton chop for lunch, a feat of endurance that gave her much gratification. In the afternoon she was rescued from a falling mast in the nick of time when *Emerald* fouled a hulk on entering harbour under tow of a steamer.

Despite sickness and danger, the Queen was a determined woman when it came to duty; the various royal yachts were made good use of in conveying her, to the cannon-roar of gun salutes on arrival and departure, around the coasts of Britain and across the Channel to the Continent. The *Royal George* finished her days at Portsmouth as a receiving hulk for the officers of the royal yachts, and was broken up in 1905. She was followed in 1843 by the first *Victoria and Albert* (a steam yacht of 1,034 tons, 225 ft in length), designed by Rear-Admiral Sir William Symonds and engined by Maudslay and Sons' double-cylinder, direct-acting engines, which drove paddle-wheels. She had one funnel and two masts and her complement was 77 officers and men plus 35 riggers from the Pembroke dockyard, where she had been built; her bunkers carried 170 tons of coal. She was first under the command of Captain Lord Adolphus Fitzclarence, a natural son of William IV.

Her maiden voyage took the royal couple on a visit to France, Queen Victoria's first experience of foreign travel and one that was to be of some diplomatic importance: this was the first time a British monarch had set foot in France on an official visit since Henry VIII had met Francis I at the Field of the Cloth of Gold in 1520. Furthermore, Anglo-French relations had been strained since 1840 when the two countries had taken opposing sides in the quarrel between Egypt and Turkey: the *Victoria and Albert* was sailing to repair the breach.

It is recorded that the Queen made a much more comfortable and luxurious voyage than had been possible in the *Royal George*. Before crossing to France the yacht cruised gently along the south coast of England to Plymouth, no doubt to give the Queen her sea-legs, calling at a number of ports *en route*, at one of which the mayor, much excited by the thought of being presented to the Queen, fell into the sea. When hauled out he was too wet and dishevelled to be presented or even to make his address of welcome.

On 2 September the *Victoria and Albert* sailed for Le Treport under escort of the royal squadron of warships, Her Majesty seated on a camp-stool on deck immediately outside the rum store and thus causing a certain dilemma for the ship's company when the pipe 'Up Spirits' was made for the drawing of the daily ration. The royal yacht was met off Le Treport by the yacht *Pluton*, carrying the Prince de Joinville, son of the French King; it is recorded that the whole visit was a great success and that it helped to create a fellowship between the two countries. When the *Victoria and Albert* cleared away finally for the return journey, the Queen was to be seen sitting on one of the paddle-boxes and graciously receiving the farewells of Napoleon III, who was waving his hand and calling his *adieus* with enthusiasm.

When a new yacht was built in 1855, the first *V and A* suffered a name-change to *Osborne*, was finally paid off in 1859 and broken up nine years later.

The new vessel, also a paddle-wheel yacht, this time with two funnels and three masts, was designed by the Controller's Department of the Admiralty and built, like her predecessor, at Pembroke in Wales; she was put into commission on 3 April 1855. Of 2,470 tons, she was 300 ft in length, with a beam just over 40 ft and a 16-ft-plus draught. She was much bigger than the first *V and A* and her speed of 14.75 knots, given by her Penn and Sons' oscillating engines, was some three knots faster. She was a supremely comfortable yacht and beautifully fitted out, with a huge complement of 240 officers and men; Queen Victoria held levées and parties aboard of much brilliance and elegance.

The royal apartments were superbly furnished: the Queen's bedroom had mahogany fittings, and her canopied bed was hung with rosebud chintz lined in green silk; green silk blinds and white muslin curtains covered the ports. Her dressing-room contained a writing-desk-cum-dressing table, and the bulkheads were lined with charts and maps operated by spring rollers. The state drawing-room, hung with chandeliers, was large for a yacht – 26 ft by 18 ft 6 in – and hung with many portraits of Victoria's large family. The furniture was of bird's-eye maple, and included an Erard piano, a bookcase and writing tables as well as two large sofas and some easy chairs. Rich curtains, also green – a strange choice for two seasick travellers – draped the corridors of all the royal apartments. There was a lords' and ladies' dining-room and twelve cabins for the royal

OPPOSITE The *Royal Escape*, in which Charles II, pursued by Oliver Cromwell after the battle of Worcester, made his escape to France. Originally a coal-brig, she was converted to become the first of many British royal yachts.

OVERLEAF Yachts of the Cumberland Fleet off St Paul's in the City of London in 1782; one of the first sailing clubs, it was founded in 1775 and was later known as the Royal Thames Yacht Club.

servants. Until 1888 light was provided by candles, but in that year the Queen gave grudging permission for electricity to be installed and 42 accumulator cells thereafter provided the illumination. This change was made on the advice of the Queen's oculist; her own inclination, as with all things, was to cherish and retain the old in preference to the new – candles having been a cherished childhood memory.

Aboard *Victoria and Albert II* the Queen witnessed the great Fleet Reviews of 1886, 1887 and 1897 – the last being the year of the Diamond Jubilee, when massed warships steamed out of Spithead past the royal yacht in salute as they made out to sea, trailing their smoke behind them until they faded into the distance; it was a huge steel armada that gladdened the old Queen's heart and brought tears to her eyes. The sailors waved their sennit hats, their cheers resounding across the water as each stately ship passed by.

In the previous year the Duke of Connaught had travelled in the royal yacht to attend the coronation of Tsar Nicholas II in St Petersburg; the *Victoria and Albert* navigated the Neva River right into the heart of the celebrating city. On 3 April 1900 the *Victoria and Albert* made her last royal voyage, sailing from Holyhead to Kingstown in Ireland in a heavy south-westerly gale. The Queen and some of the other passengers suffered badly from seasickness – nevertheless, the customary nine-course dinner continued to be served under the aegis of the royal chefs.

On 1 February 1901 the *Victoria and Albert II* had the melancholy duty of escorting the Queen's body across the Solent for her state funeral in the capital. Troops in full-dress uniform lined the route as the coffin was carried from Osborne House, where the Queen had died; it was embarked on the tender *Alberta* at Trinity Pier, East Cowes, on the Isle of Wight. *Alberta* led the sea procession, *Victoria and Albert* came immediately astern, followed by the *Osborne*, the *Hohenzollern* carrying the Queen's grandson Kaiser Wilhelm II, the *Enchantress* with the Board of Admiralty, and then the Trinity House yacht, all accompanied by eight torpedo-boat destroyers steaming ahead to form the extended naval escort. Minute guns were fired by the Fleet *en route*; at Portsmouth the Queen's body remained aboard the *Alberta* all night and next morning was borne in state to the train for London. On 3 December 1901 *Victoria and Albert II* was paid off, to be broken up and burned three years later.

Alberta, also a paddle-wheel yacht, with two funnels and three masts, was built at Pembroke and launched on 3 October 1863, commissioning at Portsmouth in the following month. Of 370 tons and capable of 14 knots, she was often used by the royal family for the short passage from Portsmouth to Cowes and acted as a tender to the *Victoria and Albert*. In 1875, when on passage from Cowes to Gosport, she had been in collision off Stokes Bay with the 120-ton schooner-rigged yacht *Mistletoe*. The Queen was much upset and urged all hands to a swift rescue of the men thrown overboard in the collision. Commander Fullerton of the *Victoria and Albert*, following astern, behaved with much gallantry, jumping into the sea in full uniform; but the yacht was a total loss and one of her crew was drowned, to the Queen's great distress. *Alberta* was broken up in 1913.

OPPOSITE, ABOVE *America*, the famous schooner-rigged yacht from New York, winning the race round the Isle of Wight in 1851 to which she gave her name.

OPPOSITE, BELOW The dining-room on the second *Victoria and Albert*, its furniture upholstered in green leather and its large windows fitted with spring-roller blinds.

ABOVE Hard tack and unruly waves led to queasiness aboard the royal yacht. In this cartoon of the 1840s Queen Victoria (to the right of centre) makes a dash for the side.

LEFT Queen Victoria's visit to Le Treport in 1843. The Queen is said to have charmed the French Emperor, Napoleon III, and to have done much for Anglo-French relations.

BELOW The Queen's bedroom in *Victoria and Albert II*, furnished in mahogany and hung with rosebud chintz.

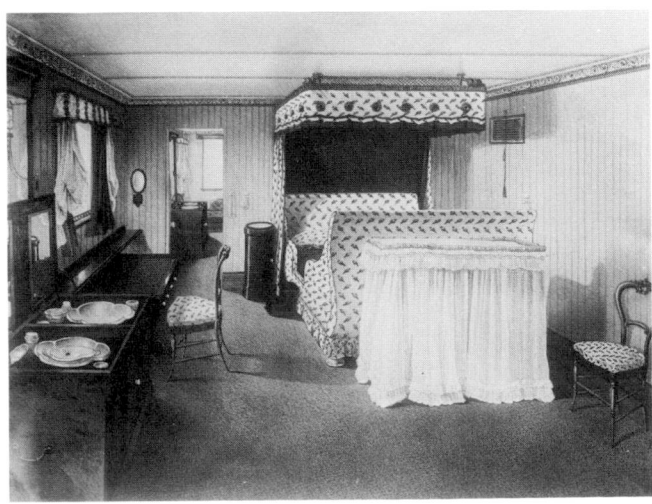

Earlier yachts of Victoria's reign included *Fairy*, a screw yacht of iron construction, 317 tons, with oscillating geared engines by Penn Brothers, built at Blackwall on the Thames and commissioned at Portsmouth in July 1845. The royal yacht tender *Elfin* was a paddle-wheel steam yacht with one funnel and two masts, commissioned at Portsmouth on 1 May 1849, built at Chatham and broken up in 1901.

The third yacht to bear the name *Victoria and Albert* was a twin-screw steamer with two bell-mouthed funnels and three raked masts; she was built at Pembroke, designed by Sir William White, KCB, and launched on 9 May 1899 by the Duchess of York (later to become Queen Mary), accompanied by the Duke of Connaught. Commissioned at Portsmouth on 23 July 1901, she was of 5,500 tons and capable of a speedy 20 knots. Her complement was 367 officers and men, plus 40 royal servants. She could steam 2,500 miles on her bunkers at her economical 14 knots.

The largest of all the world's yachts, her royal apartments were grander than any luxury yacht afloat today. On the upper deck the royal reception lobby, furnished in red morocco, dining- and smoking-rooms all had great windows – square ports – giving a magnificent all-round view. The royal dining-room was equipped to seat 30; sideboard, table and chairs were of a Hepplewhite design made in satinwood. Down through this apartment drove the mizzen-mast, while the main mast went through the smoking-room, giving the only indications, apart from the motion, of being aboard a ship at sea. On the starboard side were the King's and Queen's bedrooms and on the port side the drawing-rooms and bedrooms for other members of the royal family, plus nurseries. Royal Marines carried the food from the kitchens to the serving lift for the dining-room; the china pantry was filled with the best Crown Derby, and the glass – one of the responsibilities of the Keeper and Steward of the Royal Cabins – was of superb quality. The Royal Marines, in addition to their food-bearing duties, provided the band.

Everything on board went by established precedent: England's monarchs, at least until the advent of Edward VIII, were nothing if not conservative. Silence was the order of the day aboard: commands, which in any ordinary vessel of the Fleet would have been shouted at the highest pitch of the gunner's-mates' or boatswains' voices, were passed quietly by hand signal. Officers and seamen wore soft-soled shoes so that the heavy clump of feet should not disturb Their Majesties or their guests. At night the duty officer, in rubber soles, would silently make his rounds, seeking out potential noise be it human or cockroach.

When entering and leaving harbour there was much ceremony: on the bridge would be the Admiral, the Navigating Commander and a Lieutenant-Commander as Officer of the Watch; the First Lieutenant-Commander stood at attention, facing forward, at the heel of the bowsprit on the topgallant fo'c'sle, with another Lieutenant-Commander in general charge aft. When passing other ships there would be bugle salutes and piping parties, and when entering or leaving harbour the gun salutes boomed and roared amid much smoke from the saluting batteries ashore.

In her long career this great vessel cruised with her different monarchs

RIGHT The Naval Review, 3 July 1897: *Victoria and Albert II* passing through the lines of the Fleet.

BELOW A distant view of the Fleet's night-time illuminations at Spithead. Long lines of battleships and cruisers, many with famous names, afterwards steamed past the Queen who watched from the royal yacht.

to Lisbon, Copenhagen, Cherbourg, the Norwegian fiords and the western Mediterranean, including such ports as Piraeus, Toulon, Corfu, Gibraltar and Venice. In 1905 the *Entente Cordiale*, Edward VII's great dream of the establishment of harmony with his neighbours, was much cemented by a joint review from the *Victoria and Albert* of the combined French and British Fleets, the former under the command of Vice-Admiral Caillard, the latter under Admiral Sir Arthur Wilson. In the following year the King and Queen visited the Mediterranean, spending a week in Athens, afterwards cruising the Greek coast to Katakolo with the Greek royal family embarked as guests. In 1908 she took Edward VII to Reval on a visit to the Russian Emperor. During the First World War she was laid up, but returned once more to service when peace came, although she was not used again as frequently as before. Nevertheless, she was a welcome sight at the Fleet Review of 1935 on the occasion of George V's Silver Jubilee, and again in 1937 for the coronation of George VI, when a huge concourse of ships – the last time a great assembly of capital ships was to be reviewed – lay ready for the King, who was wearing the uniform of Admiral of the Fleet: battleships, battle-cruisers – among them *HMS Hood*, later to be lost in the Denmark Strait – aircraft-carriers, cruisers, destroyers and submarines stood at anchor, each ship's company cheering as the *Victoria and Albert* passed down the lines.

Last of her name, *Victoria and Albert III* was not replaced until Queen Elizabeth II came to the throne in 1953, though 1937 marked her last official appearance.

Yachting was one of the many interests of Edward VII, both as Prince of Wales and as King; in 1907 *Victoria and Albert* was present in the Isle of Wight for Cowes Week when the King sailed his racing yacht *Britannia* and watched the race for the King's Cup, which was won by the German Emperor's yacht *Meteor*. From 1882 to 1901 Edward was Commodore of the Royal Yacht Squadron; on ascending the throne he became the first Admiral of the Squadron, an honour that later went to his son George V. Edward owned, besides the splendid *Britannia*, seven smaller yachts: *Dagmar*, 36 tons, built in 1886, *Princess* 1869, *Alexandra* 1871, *Zenobia* 1872, *Hildegarde* 1876, *Formosa* 1880 and *Aline* 1882. The King's nephew Wilhelm II of Germany was also keenly interested in the great schooner-rigged racers, though possibly his interest was due more to his wish to encourage his people to become sea-minded than to pure sporting instincts. Nevertheless, he disliked losing (and was not, in truth, much of a sportsman). In 1893, when the Kaiser's *Meteor I* and Lord Dunraven's *Valkyrie* were in competition during Cowes Week for the Queen's Cup, there was an unsavoury incident: the German Emperor alleged that the winning *Valkyrie* had passed on the wrong side of the mark, disregarding the fact that the usual mark had been replaced by the Bullock Patch buoy, as he very well knew. This was a frivolous complaint, but to avoid unpleasantness Lord Dunraven (himself a holder of a Board of Trade Extra Master's certificate) waived his claim to the award; the German Emperor thus won not only the trophy but also the contempt of the yachting community. It was largely as a result of this fracas – not helped when the Kaiser let it be known that he regarded all rules as inoperable against Germany – that his long-suffering uncle the Prince of Wales withdrew for some years from the racing scene and sold *Britannia*, though she was later to come back into royal ownership.

The Kaiser was the first owner of the cutter *Thistle*. When *Thistle* was soundly thrashed by both *Britannia* and *Valkyrie* he had a new yacht designed by the great G.L.Watson; but when it proved unsuitable he gave it away; in 1896 he took delivery of the cutter *Meteor II*, designed once again by Watson and built at Henderson's yard. Although a great success she was to be replaced by *Sabyrite*, and, renamed *Orion*, she passed into German Naval service.

The schooner *Westward*, designed in 1904 by the noted American designer Herreshoff for A.S.Cochrane, was later bought by a German syndicate after successful racing at Kiel. Renamed *Hamburg II*, she was used by the Kaiser in his racing stable. At this time there was great rivalry between Britain and Germany in yacht racing, and at Kiel Regatta in 1913 the British *Margherita*, skippered by the famous 'Shrimp' Embling, raced *Meteor*, *Westward* and *Germania*, which belonged to Krupp, the arms manufacturer. Much to the Kaiser's annoyance she won five firsts. *Margherita* was later sold to Sir William Reardon Smith (of Smith's of Cardiff, noted tramp-steamer owners) for use in training seamen; renamed *Davida*, her rig was altered and she was fitted with auxiliary diesels. These and many others of the day – notably the American schooner *Suzanne* – were vessels of great beauty and character and most were to have long careers, though not exclusively in racing.

As regards state yachts, things were somewhat different in America. It was said that the American presidents of the nineteenth century allowed their rich citizens to sail in rather more style than they did themselves; certainly, the first of the presidential yachts was nothing spectacular. It must be admitted, however, that presidents of the United States had not the same need for yachts as had, for instance, the kings and queens of Britain; most presidential travelling was done by the railroad that was soon to traverse the great land mass of America from coast to coast and from north to south. That was really all that was needed and the sea was of secondary importance.

The first yacht was the *River Queen*, a steamer of 536 tons. Used by President Lincoln, she was in fact a vessel rented from a private owner, George N. Power; it was aboard the *River Queen* that Lincoln, on 3 February 1865, held a vital conference with the Peace Commission of the Confederacy, thus taking the first faltering steps towards the modern constitution of the United States. In 1873 the president was accorded his own yacht, when the *Despatch* was bought by the US Navy for the joint use of themselves and the president.

Despatch was a somewhat ungainly vessel of 560 tons, rigged as a brigantine and mechanically propelled by a single screw. She was in fact little used on presidential duties other than a number of cruises on the Potomac, where President Hayes and his vice-president held many parties aboard. She was finally wrecked, coming to grief on the coast of Virginia.

OPPOSITE The Prince and Princess of Wales in 1898, watching the Cowes scene from *Victoria and Albert*, in rather greater elegance than is possible today.

Next came a yacht both finer and larger: the *Dolphin*, a 1,465-ton three-masted screw schooner built in 1884 in Chester, Pennsylvania, and also used on combined presidential and naval duties; and she was often the carrier of important foreign visitors as guests of the president. In use at the same time was *Sylph*, a screw schooner, much smaller at 152 tons, shared by the president and the Secretary of the Navy and much used by Presidents Taft, MacKinley and Theodore Roosevelt. A good-looking vessel with elegant lines, she was a favourite of Roosevelt's.

In 1902 *Mayflower* came into use for presidential duties. Designed by G. L. Watson and Clyde-built in 1896, she was of 1,806 tons, 275 ft long, with two masts, a long bowsprit and a single funnel – all very symmetrical – and was propelled by two triple-expansion engines giving her 16·5 knots. She undertook many naval duties, serving at one time as flagship of the US North Atlantic Fleet under Admiral Dewey and later as flagship in the Mediterranean and the Caribbean; Theodore Roosevelt was aboard her when peace terms were agreed in 1905 between Japan and Russia. Earlier, *Mayflower* had seen active service in the Spanish-American War, having been present at the blockade against Cuba. Laid up by order of President Hoover as a measure of economy, she was later sold after suffering fire damage in Philadelphia in 1931. But she was taken back into service during the Second World War, when she joined the Coastguard. She was to be the last of the large presidential steam yachts, diesel being preferred and the yachts becoming very much smaller.

As in Britain, foreign royalties maintained luxury vessels for use on great occasions of state as well as for pleasure and relaxation, and in most cases the vessels concerned were a charge upon the country's naval service and could be used as despatch vessels or hospital ships in time of war.

Britain's greatest yachting rival before the First World War was Germany: Wilhelm II, grandson of Victoria, nephew of Edward VII and cousin of George V first brought power politics into sport; he saw yachting through the eyes of Mars – as a means of increasing his people's awareness of the important part a strong German Navy could play in war. His feelings against Britain were already strong; for one thing, Victoria was a tiresome grandmother for a grown man; for another he could not resist poking fun at his Uncle Edward. It was a source of glee to the Kaiser that his third racing yacht, *Meteor II*, built in 1896 by Henderson on the Clyde – the builders who had produced *Britannia* – was a foot longer than his uncle's, and that her sail area was greater by 2,000 sq ft. *Meteor II* shone brilliantly in the '96 season, outracing *Britannia*. In the following year her fortunes changed, but, when converted to yawl rig in 1899, she won splendid victories in Cowes Week; the Kaiser seemed set to be hailed as the world's most successful yachtsman. He then acquired *Meteor III*, a 412-ton schooner, a vast racer indeed, product of Carey Smith of America. His ambitions were boundless: he persuaded his industrialists to build yachts, set up a training scheme to teach his young men the art of handling sail, and, determined to bring Germany to the forefront of yacht building and design, he encouraged the inflow of builders and designers from

America and Britain. The Kaiser was a frequent attender at regattas in the Baltic, and became a member of the (British) Royal Yacht Squadron, coming over in his state yacht for Cowes Week to ensure the superiority of the German Empire in British waters.

Wilhelm II had inherited the paddle-schooner *Hohenzollern* (later *Kaiseradler*), laid down by the North German Shipbuilding Company at Kiel in 1875, some 13 years before his accession to the throne, and completed in 1876. She was a large yacht: 1,707 tons, 268 ft overall, beam 33 ft, draught 14 ft. Her complement was 145 officers and men. Two-masted, with a long bowsprit and clipper bow, her hull was of iron and her paddles churned her through the water at 15 knots. In addition, she carried 3,560 ft of steadying sail. Her iron sides were broken by large square gunports; she had a brace of bell-mouthed funnels and two 3.4-in guns. Also for royal use was the *Royal Louise*, a sailing frigate presented years before by William IV of England to Frederick William III of Germany.

The Kaiser had been taken as a child in 1869 to Wilhelmshaven by his father, and there for the first time he saw a warship – the *König Wilhelm*, biggest in the German Fleet; it was this impressive sight of gun-power that first gave him his lifelong desire for a powerful navy.

In 1893 the Vulcan Shipbuilding Company built at Stettin a new and larger *Hohenzollern*, ordered to the specifications of the German Admiralty. This new yacht took the place of the old *Hohenzollern*, which was now renamed *Kaiseradler* and earmarked for the use of the Crown Prince – 'Little Willy' as he was to become known to the British troops in the Great War. The Kaiser gloried in his new yacht. Of 3,775 tons, she was steel-hulled, 382 ft in length with a 45-ft 9-in beam and 23-ft draught. She was capable of 21.5 knots from her two triple-expansion engines by Vulcan-Stettin, their steam produced by eight Scotch boilers. *Hohenzollern* was a splendid yacht, admirably fitted for any emperor; but it came as some surprise to the German Admiralty that His Majesty expected the sole use of the great new ship. She had been intended for use by the Navy as a despatch vessel, and it was only when he performed the launching ceremony that the Kaiser made it very clear that she was, in fact, to be his private yacht.

He was now well in advance as regards the European royal yacht league, having overtaken the Queen's *Victoria and Albert II* along with all the others. *Hohenzollern*, with her great ram surmounted by the crest of the Imperial Eagle and much gilded work, delighted Wilhelm. He loved being at sea in her, and used to gaze for hours from the bridge, especially in starry Scandinavian waters at night, when he would dream of German naval power. *Hohenzollern* was also to be seen sailing majestically in the Baltic, the Adriatic, the Mediterranean and the North Sea (to the Germans, the German Ocean) sometimes with a warship escort. One of the things the Kaiser was said to have liked about life aboard was the fact that he was isolated from affairs of state and could not be 'got at', while free to transmit his own orders at will. He was often accompanied by congenial guests, mainly generals of his army – Prince Philipp zee Eulenberg, General von Chelius of the Guards Hussars, his ADC General von Halinke, and General von Kessel.

RIGHT A racing scene aboard the German Emperor's yacht *Meteor*.

BELOW Nicholas II, Tsar of all the Russias, with, to the right, Kaiser Wilhelm II of Germany.

BELOW RIGHT The German Emperor's steam yacht *Hohenzollern* at Cowes Week, 1894. Of 3,775 tons and steel built, she was intended as a despatch vessel for the German Navy but was appropriated by the Kaiser for his personal use. Driven by twin screws, she was capable of 21·5 knots.

It was Wilhelm II's dream that the annual Kiel Week should outshine the British Cowes Week. But Kiel was all too militaristic, having none of the charm, gaiety and informality of Cowes. Kiel Regatta was a thing of many court and official functions and dinners, of much splendour – and even more boasting, the Kaiser hoping to use the event to help stimulate his nation's interest in achieving a stronger navy. Usually the existing might of the German Navy was at Kiel for all the world to see and marvel at: lines of battleships and battle-cruisers, flotillas of destroyers and sub-marines that eventually were to be sent to meet the British Fleet in war. That was Kiel: a naval and military occasion first and foremost; thus, although there was much social glitter, famous names and great yachtsmen, it was never quite Cowes. There were too many brass bands, admirals and goose-stepping soldiers, busy naval launches, and the humourless, uniformed Kaiser scowling when his yachts lost their races. There were yachts, both racing and cruising, from half the world – America, Britain, Italy, France, Norway, Spain; at the 1912 Regatta many of the great transatlantic liners were also present, on charter to German wealth, to act as grandstands for the privileged spectators, dressed overall with gay coloured bunting like the German warships, while overhead flew aeroplanes and zeppelins. Almost all the world's best racers had entered for the 24 events; sadly for the Kaiser, victory went to only nine German entries.

Wilhelm II was keen to improve relations with the Tsar of All The Russias, Nicholas II. In July 1905 there was a meeting between the two Emperors, Wilhelm sailing to Bjorko in Russian waters aboard *Hohenzollern* and Nicholas joining him in his royal yacht *Polar Star*. The Kaiser was invited aboard for luncheon; all went well and that same day both Emperors signed a treaty of friendship known as the Treaty of Bjorko; alas, it proved meaningless, as it was not ratified by the Kaiser's advisers on his return and never came into force. After this, the royal yachts of Germany and Russia figured in two more equally abortive meetings – at Swinemund and Port Baltic, the former in filthy weather, good neither for the Tsar's sto-mach (Nicholas was sick every time he went to sea) nor for the Kaiser's complimentary Russian uniform, soaked when he was transferred to the Tsar's vessel at anchor. Meanwhile, the Kaiser's naval ideas were growing apace; the waves were there to be ruled, and Britain had been at it long enough. As the nineteenth century ran to its close he sent a remarkably boastful telegram to Tsar Nicholas as from the 'Admiral of the Western Ocean' to the Admiral of the eastern one. The only reaction of the British Admiralty to this self-assumption was a shrug of the shoulders and a remark to the effect that so far as they knew, Admiral Lord Fisher was still in charge westerly.

By 1913 *Hohenzollern* had been surpassed in size by both the new *Victoria and Albert III* and by the Russian Tsar's *Standart*, and the Kaiser's nose was out of joint. Although he laid down an immense yacht of some-thing over 7,000 tons by way of revenge, her building was overtaken by the outbreak of war; it was while the Kaiser was aboard *Hohenzollern* at the Kiel Regatta in late June 1914, with his yacht dressed overall in honour of the splendid occasion, that a telegram was delivered to him saying that Archduke Franz Ferdinand of Austria had been assassinated at Sarajevo. The Kaiser cancelled the Regatta, lowered the Imperial Standard to half mast, and returned at once to Potsdam. Leaving Potsdam again on 6 July for a cruise in Scandinavian waters, he sent orders from *Hohenzollern* for the German Fleet to move from Jutland to their bases at Kiel and Wilhelmshaven. When he was given news that the British Fleet was steaming from the Spithead review to what looked like their war stations, he ordered *Hohenzollern* back to Kiel. The stage was set for war.

The Tsar of All the Russias was as anxious to attain maritime superiority over Great Britain as was the German Emperor, and, like Wilhelm II, Alexander II saw the prestige of a great yacht as a way towards this end. In 1880 the Govan yard of John Elder built the triple-screw steam yacht *Livadia* of no less than 11,000 tons, 266 ft in length with a huge 153-ft beam. This was a most splendid royal yacht, regal in her appointments if of unorthodox Russian Admiralty design; this gave her a curious and topheavy aspect and a duck-like progress through the water – for she was not far off spherical. Other unusual features were the goal-post foremast, foreshadowing the ocean-going freighters of a later age, and the subdivision of her double bottoms into watertight compartments, which was uncommon at that time. Her unwieldy, matronly roundness kept her mostly in the Black Sea, where the Tsar (assassinated before she arrived in Sevastopol) had intended to make use of her as a palace upon the waters rather than venture too far beyond the Bosphorus. Splendidly fitted out, with marble mosaic alleyways and a fountain set in the main saloon amid beds of flowers, she had a 12-ft clearance between her two main decks. However, she was never put to much use and was broken up in 1926 in the port of her first arrival in Russian waters.

In 1888 the Russian-built twin-screw schooner *Poliarnaia Zvesda*, much smaller at 3,270 tons, replaced the *Livadia*. More conventional, she had a 46-ft beam and a length of 336 ft: roundness was out. Tsar Alexander III and his family took a cruise each year in the Baltic, but this apart, she too was little used. In 1895 a Copenhagen yard, Burmeister and Wain, produced another twin-screw steam schooner, the stately black-hulled *Standart* of 4,500 tons with a speed of 18 knots, to the annoyance of the German Kaiser and the pleasure (if pleasure it was, considering his stomach) of another new Tsar, Nicholas II, who had ascended the throne the year before. *Standart* was a finely proportioned vessel with two white funnels and three masts, as in the case of *Poliarnaia Zvesda*; again her fittings were magnificent and this time a children's room and even a chapel were included in her accommodation. There were canvas awnings in plenty, and wicker chairs and tables lined the gleaming, spotless decks. The drawing-rooms and dining-rooms below, beautifully panelled in mahogany, were lit by crystal chandeliers. A platoon of the Imperial Marine Guards was normally embarked, while the vessel carried her own balalaika orchestra and a military brass band. Very often there were royal children aboard, for Nicholas thoroughly enjoyed his annual family cruises off Finland. Each child was placed in the personal charge of one

RIGHT The Imperial Russian steam yacht *Standart*, pride of Tsar Nicholas II. He made much use of her and frequently cruised in Finnish waters, despite his seasickness.

BELOW The Tsar with his mother, Marie Fedorovna, and his daughters, Olga, Tatiana, Marie and Anastasia, on the deck of *Standart* in 1913.

of *Standart*'s seamen, whose duty it was to keep the child safe, aboard and ashore, his reward being a gold watch presented by the Tsar as each June cruise came to an end.

Nicholas did much work aboard his yacht, and routine reports similar to the Queen of England's despatches reached him daily. *Standart* was an impressive sight, with her big gold-encrusted bowsprit, especially when, for special occasions, her masts were decorated with coloured flags and pennants. She was very much in use for the conduct of international affairs: in 1897 Felix Fauré, President of the French Republic, had a meeting with Nicholas II on board the yacht, even her weather decks being carpeted for the occasion, and it was then that the Franco-Russian alliance was cemented. There were frequent meetings with the German Emperor – kinsman, via the ubiquitous Queen Victoria, of the Tsar. *Standart* was present, with the Tsar to take the salute, when in 1904 the Russian Fleet under Admiral Rozhdestvensky sailed for the world flag-showing cruise; this event was largely instigated by the Kaiser, but it ceased when the Russian ships were destroyed in the war against Japan by the Japanese Admiral Togo in the Tsushima Strait.

In August 1909 the *Standart* brought Nicholas to England and Cowes Regatta; there, in the uniform of a British admiral, he carried out a review of the British Fleet at Spithead in company with Edward VII and later took part in the glittering dinner-parties and balls of Cowes Week. In June 1914 *Standart* took the Russian royal family to Constanza on the Black Sea, where they met King Carol of Rumania with the object of arranging a marriage between the King and the Tsar's 18-year-old daughter, the Grand Duchess Olga; it is recorded that when this proved a fruitless voyage, no-one was more relieved than Olga herself. At the end of June, at Kronstadt in the Baltic, Nicholas reviewed Britain's First Battle-Cruiser Squadron under Vice-Admiral Sir David Beatty, the *Lion*, the *Queen Mary*, the *New Zealand* and the *Princess Royal* steaming in might and majesty past the Russian royal yacht to their anchorage – after which Nicholas and his family lunched aboard Beatty's flagship.

As in the case of the Kaiser aboard *Hohenzollern*, it was aboard *Standart* that Nicholas II, a sick man by now, heard the news from Sarajevo of the assassination of Archduke Franz Ferdinand; on the following day came the even more startling news that Rasputin, the 'mad monk', confidant of the Tsarina, had suffered an attempt on his life.

After the Revolution *Standart* was taken into the Soviet Navy, and in 1960 was still serving as a minelayer, under the name of *Marti*.

Other nations too aspired to royal or state splendour in their yacht-building. The Austro-Hungarian Empire under the Emperor Franz Joseph produced the 330-ton paddle-yacht *Fantasie* in 1857, London-built, 176 ft in length with a 16-ft beam, a graceful vessel with a long bow and bowsprit. She was used chiefly on the Danube, though it is believed that she carried the Emperor to Egypt in 1869 for the inauguration of the Suez Canal. She remained in use until the *Miramar* was built in 1872, another paddle-yacht, this time of 1,830 tons, from Samauda Brothers of London, who had built *Fantasie*.

Belgium produced the handsome 1,322-ton twin-screw schooner *Alberta* in 1896. Built at Troon in Scotland, she carried two masts on a steel hull and had a speed of 17 knots. She had been ordered originally for A. J. Drexel, an American tycoon, under the name of *Margarita*. Leopold II put her in permanent moorings at Cap Ferrat, using her principally as an office; he was an eccentric rather than a seadog. She scarcely went to sea again until she was taken into Russian naval service after the end of the First World War, passing afterwards to the British Navy as *HMS Surprise*, and as such took part in the Second World War.

The Danes, ever a seafaring race, built the *Elephenten* for the use of Christian V as early as 1687. She was a two-masted vessel with fore-and-aft rig (yacht sails as opposed to the square rig of warships), and very ornately decorated, especially in the royal apartments aft. She was also equipped with small guns. In 1690 the larger *Cronen* replaced her. In 1845 came steam and the three-masted paddle-schooner *Slesvig* of 740 tons, built as the *Copenhagen* and becoming the royal yacht in 1856 after service in the Danish Navy. In 1879 she was replaced by the larger and much more impressive *Dannebrog*, also a paddle-schooner, whose elegance, though not her size, put her almost in the class of the British *Victoria and Albert* of the same period. In her the King and Queen of Denmark paid a state visit to Britain in 1914, entering the Medway through lines of British warships.

In France the royal yacht contender was *L'Aigle*, a paddle-schooner of some 160 ft in length. Built in 1858 for Louis Napoleon, *L'Aigle* was a sturdy and well-fitted vessel with a bell-mouthed funnel and three masts, plus imitation gunports such as had many ships of the period. In her the Empress Eugenie attended the opening of the Suez Canal in 1869 – in fact, as befitted the mother country of de Lesseps, *L'Aigle* led the procession of ships through the canal. In 1859 was built *Jerome Napoleon*, a screw barquentine, not a particularly beautiful vessel but useful for carrying the various French royals on their ceremonial occasions. After her came *La Reine Hortense*, another screw barquentine which conveyed the royal family to Cowes Week, Napoleon III being a member of the Royal Yacht Squadron. But this was to be France's last royal yacht, for Napoleon was shortly afterwards relieved of his throne.

In Italy, in 1883, Victor Emmanuel II built the screw barquentine *Savoia I*, large for those days at 3,266 tons. This vessel was in service as a royal yacht until 1902 after which she became a floating workshop for the Italian Navy. In 1900 the ex-British merchantman *America*, renamed *Trinacria*, came into royal use and proved a most impressive ship for her duties. She carried an exceptionally large complement and some useful armament. She was replaced in 1925, under Mussolini, by *Savoia II*, a twin-screw schooner of 4,388 tons capable of 22 knots. She had been built at the Royal Arsenal in Spezia under the name *Cita di Palermo*. Apart from her royal duties for the King, she was used as Mussolini's showboat for the Fascist regime.

In her day the most luxurious of royal yachts, she was sunk by bombs in the Adriatic whilst on service in the Second World War.

Holland, progenitor of the *jaghts* or yachts that came to Britain on the restoration of Charles II to the throne, should not have hung back in the royal yacht stakes, yet the fact remains that the first of her royal yachts was a strange-looking vessel, the *De Leeuw*, a paddle-steamer of somewhat hedgehog-like aspect which carried only one tall, thin funnel and a skimpy foremast. She was ornately decorated, the royal Dutch arms magnificent upon the paddle-boxes, and she boasted a gallery aft, similar to the admiral's quarters aboard a man-o'-war, with a poop-deck above. Her figurehead was a lion, giving her a ferocious aspect bows-on. She gave 55 years of sea service to the King, and she was finally replaced by *De Valk* in 1882 – a paddle-schooner of only marginally more pleasing looks, though she was bigger and faster and of a more conventional design, with two funnels and two nicely proportioned masts. William II of the Netherlands, as a member of the Royal Yacht Squadron, brought *De Valk* to Cowes on a number of occasions. She was returned from the royal service in 1890 and no new yacht was commissioned until *Piet Hein*, a twin-screw motor yacht of 151 tons, was built in 1937 and presented as a wedding gift to the future Queen, Juliana.

Amphion, a schooner built in Sweden in 1778, was much used by Gustav III for his cruises, mostly in the Finnish Archipelago and on Lake Malaren, where her shallow draught was a useful asset. Her sails were assisted by oar-power – which raises interesting visions of galley-slaves. She remained in the King's service until he died in 1792, when she was relegated to the status of a depot ship and survived as such until 1885. In 1887 the screw schooner *Drott* was built. *Drott* was of 630 tons and could steam at 12 knots. With her two masts, two funnels and iron hull, she was a graceful-looking vessel, in many respects ahead of her time, and followed the pattern of much later craft in the shape of her stem, the conventional clipper bow being discarded in favour of a straight stem.

The screw schooner *Amelia II* was built in 1880 for Prince Carlos of Portugal, who had previously owned the smaller *Amelia*, first of the name. The Prince came to the throne as Carlos I in 1889 and subsequently owned *Amelia III*, a twin-screw schooner of 900 tons which had first belonged to Colonel Harry MacCalmont under the name *Banshee*. *Amelia III*, more like a warship than a yacht, had the sad duty in 1910 of carrying the royal family to Gibraltar, and exile, after the proclamation of the Portuguese Republic.

Colonel MacCalmont supplied another royal yacht, this time to Spain in 1898: *Giralda*, a twin-screw schooner of 1,664 tons. Like so many other royals, Alphonso XIII was a member of the Royal Yacht Squadron and *Giralda* was much seen at Cowes during the week of the Regatta. Built by the Fairfield Shipbuilding and Engineering Co. at Glasgow, *Giralda*, when owned by MacCalmont, was the first private (as opposed to royal)

RIGHT The paddle yacht *Fantasie*, built in London in 1857 for Emperor Franz Joseph of Austria. *Fantasie* is thought to have taken him to Egypt for the opening of the Suez Canal.

BELOW A procession of ships, led by the French paddle schooner *L'Aigle* carrying the Empress Eugenie, opened the Suez Canal in 1869.

yacht of more than 1,000 tons; she was very spacious inside, though modest enough when compared with the great royal vessels of Britain, Germany and Russia.

In 1904 *Erthogroul* was built for the Sultan of Turkey by Armstrong Whitworth on the Tyne. A twin-screw schooner, she was a nicely proportioned vessel of 964 tons, 264 ft in length with two funnels, three raked masts and an elegant clipper bow. She passed on to Sultan Mohamed v and was known to be in his service until 1918.

3 Millionaires and their Steam Yachts

In the early days, steam as a means of propulsion was much frowned upon: no sensible person would go to sea in a vessel without sails, and those who used auxiliary steam could not strictly be considered gentlemen. Steam meant coal, and coal and smoke were dirty. The Royal Yacht Squadron turned up its collective nose, notwithstanding the fact that as far back as 1819 an American, Colonel Stevens, had taken the engine-equipped *Savannah* across the North Atlantic, though certainly he had relied more upon sail than upon the new-fangled steam. It was not until 1853 that all steam limiting rules were rescinded by the Royal Yacht Squadron, though nine years earlier they had admitted steamers to membership as long as they were over 100 h.p.

Lord Brassey and Sunbeam

Thomas Brassey, born at Stafford in 1836, the son of a well-known railway contractor and engineer, was one of the earliest owners of steam vessels. He became Liberal Member of Parliament for Devonport in 1865, and for Hastings from 1868 to 1886 – both seafaring constituencies. Raised to the peerage in 1886, he became a Civil Lord of the Admiralty and later Secretary to the Admiralty, and was known as an authority on naval matters. Brassey was also chairman of the Opium Commission, and other commissions of such diverse character as those for unseaworthy ships, coaling-stations, and pensions for the aged poor; he was also President of the Institute of Naval Architects.

During 1876–7 Brassey, with his wife and four children, circumnavigated the globe in his 170-ft screw composite three-masted topsail schooner *Sunbeam*, a splendid, shapely vessel of 576 tons designed by St Clare Byrne of Liverpool and built by Bowdler, Chaffer and Company on the Mersey in 1874. Her engines, by Laird, produced 350 h.p., giving a maximum speed of 10·13 knots and an economical cruising speed of eight knots, the latter consuming four tons of coal a day. She could remain at sea without bunkering for around eleven days, which gave her a good deal of cruising scope.

Sunbeam left Chatham on 1 July 1876 and cleared away from Cowes

ABOVE *Sunbeam*, a three-masted topsail schooner built for Thomas Brassey.

BELOW LEFT Thomas Brassey, who sailed *Sunbeam* on a world cruise in 1876–7. BELOW *Sunbeam* under shortened sail in Sogne Fiord, Norway.

for Ushant on 6 July with 43 people aboard, the guest list including a Captain of the Royal Naval Reserve and a Commander of the Royal Navy. Among the 34 crew members were a sailing master, a surgeon, a bosun, a carpenter, a signalman/gunner, coxswains of the gig and cutter, a captain of the hold, 11 common seamen, two engineers, two stokers, a cook for the fo'c'sle hands and four stewards; for the guests there was another cook and a mate, a nurse, a lady's maid and a stewardess. *Sunbeam* travelled 35,400 miles of ocean on her world cruise, spending a total of 112 days in various harbours; she visited Madeira, Teneriffe, the Cape Verde Islands, Rio de Janeiro, Monte Video and Buenos Aires, and navigated the Strait of Magellan and the Smith Channel to Valparaiso before moving on across the Pacific. Whilst on the coast of Patagonia she rescued the crew of 15 hands from the barque *Monkshaven*; laden with an inflammable cargo of smelting coal, she had been on fire for six days before *Sunbeam* found her.

The yacht was richly and heavily furnished and decorated in the contemporary style, with ornate mantelpieces around the fireplaces, fussy lamps and oddments – china plates, pictures, knick-knacks – fixed to the bulkheads: a floating home from home. The fo'c'sle hands lived mainly in deckhouses swept, as in any ordinary merchant ship of the period, by spray and solid water when a gale blew up. These men were mainly fishermen from the Essex coast, trained among the banks and shoals at the mouth of the Thames – most of them related by blood or marriage to the sailing master, Isaiah Powell. On his return from his world cruise, Brassey wrote a letter, published in *The Times* on 2 June 1877, describing his seafaring experiences and drawing certain conclusions in regard to the dangers of the ocean and the causes of past marine disasters: he attributed them largely to negligence, offering it as his opinion that safe navigation was perfectly possible in any water and under any conditions so long as proper prudence was maintained – a blanket conclusion with which many mariners might well disagree.

Sunbeam herself had had her share of misadventure: at Yokohama fire had broken out aboard owing to the nursery coals being made up dangerously high one cold night; on another occasion the yacht was attacked in Chinese waters by pirates, wild men who made an attempt to board but who were driven away by the use of the deck hoses. On subsequent cruises Brassey's guest list included Lord Tennyson and the grand old man of British politics, William Ewart Gladstone.

Sir Thomas Lipton

Thomas Johnstone Lipton was born in Glasgow in 1850, the son of poor Irish parents; at the age of nine he started work as an errand boy for his father, who ran a small grocery shop. At 15 he emigrated as a steerage passenger to America, where for some five years he worked as a tram driver, a labourer on a plantation and as a grocer's assistant. When he returned to Glasgow he went back to grocery and a year later was able to open his own business – a small provision store. Ten years later he owned a string of shops all over the United Kingdom. He bought extensively overseas: a packing-house for pigs in Chicago, tea and coffee plantations in Ceylon, while developing bacon-curing, fruit farming and baking businesses at home.

Lipton was a sportsman through and through, a generous man who never lost his early love for the sea and the open air, despite the intense pressures of his vast business interests and the long, hard climb from poverty in the back streets of Glasgow to the pinnacles of fame and success. Always interested in yachting and the great contests for the America's Cup, he decided, when he was in a financial position to do so, to enter for the race himself; accordingly the first *Shamrock*, a superb 129-ft yacht (refitted in 1979 at a cost of around a million pounds and renamed *Quadrifoglio*) was built in 1899 by Thorneycroft to William Fife's design. She was followed by a succession of *Shamrocks*; and although after five attempts Lipton never did win back the Cup for Britain, he earned tremendous respect on both sides of the Atlantic for his tenacity and good humour.

'Tea Tom' (as opposed to his friend 'Whisky Tom' Dewar) was perhaps one of the best loved, admired and respected of all the yachtsmen of his time, in spite of his extraordinary flair for publicity. But although he was a personal friend of Edward VII, both as Prince of Wales and as King, it proved impossible for many years to put up his name for the Royal Yacht Squadron. Its members were bitterly opposed to him on account of the way he was said to have used yachting as a means of propagating the gospel of Lipton's Tea in the United States. Nor was a certain voyage aboard the liner *Oratava* to Ceylon easily forgotten or forgiven. Some of the ship's baled cargo had had to be jettisoned after an unfortunate grounding in the Red Sea, and Lipton, cajoling a crew member into cutting him a stencil, was to be found painting DRINK LIPTON'S TEA on to the cast-away bales in the hope that they would float into areas of the world where his empire had not yet been established. Enterprising, perhaps, but the liner's captain was much displeased by such opportunism. So badly did the crowned heads of Europe take to the idea of trade entering a gentleman's sport that the Kaiser was heard to refer acidly to the fact that the King of England had taken to going sailing with his grocer.

Lipton's interest in the sea was not confined to sailing and racing: he owned one of the finest and biggest steam yachts of the day – *Erin*, built in 1896 under the name *Aegusa* and intended for an Italian owner. *Erin* displaced 1,330 tons and her overall length was 287 ft; her 4-cylinder triple-expansion engine gave her 15·6 knots via a single screw. She made many cruises to the Mediterranean, often carrying the King's mistress Mrs Keppel as a guest, Lipton in his turn being entertained aboard the royal yacht *Victoria and Albert*. *Erin* was the last word in comfort and opulence and her interior was striking: watercolours by de Martino and Parker Newton adorned the bulkheads; the music-room contained brasses, bronzes, ormolu, buhl, blue Sèvres vases, even a harp. The great saloon was magnificent at night beneath blue lampshades, the table glittering with silver, crystal and the jewels of splendidly dressed women. These guests, largely from the British upper crust, attended a formal dinner every night at 9 p.m. When weather permitted, luncheon tables capable of accommodating 70 people were set up on deck. The owner's and guests' staterooms were fitted with gilded beds, with wash-stands that also did duty as desks,

ABOVE An advertisement for the tea which brought Thomas Lipton his fortune.

RIGHT Sir Thomas Lipton, one of the most famous names in yachting history.

BELOW The magnificent steam yacht *Erin*, owned by Lipton and often used as escort for his racing yachts when they crossed the Atlantic to challenge for the America's Cup.

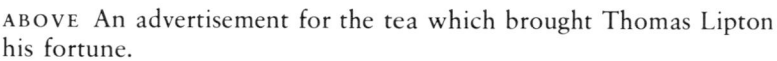

and rich carpets. At tea-time – Lipton gave lavish tea parties, always at 3 p.m. – tea was freshly made for each guest, even for each cup. Hot crumpets and broiled birds were served with champagne, and there was a gift for every guest. Some 3,000 lamps lit the vessel at night when in port.

Lipton was aboard *Erin* in New York when Admiral Dewey of the US Navy entered in honour and glory aboard his flagship *Olympia*, after destroying a number of enemy vessels in Manila during the Spanish-American War which had just ended. New York was *en fête*; the huge procession of yachts and steam vessels which had turned out to welcome Dewey was led on the port column by *Erin*, while the starboard column was led by *Corsair* belonging to J.P. Morgan, a fellow millionaire. Later in the proceedings, which included a great parade of the cadets from the military academy at West Point with Governor Roosevelt present, Lipton accompanied Dewey to the triumphal arch in Madison Square and the saluting base. The reason: tea. *Olympia* had called at Colombo on her way back to the States, and packets of Lipton's Tea were given to each member of the ship's company. No doubt this gesture appealed to the Admiral's sense of humour as well as eliciting his gratitude. The sage gentlemen of the Royal Yacht Squadron across the Atlantic must have shaken their heads and muttered. Tea, after all, was still trade.

In 1914, whilst on passage to the United States in company with *Shamrock IV*, *Erin*'s radio intercepted a message from one German cruiser to another which stated that war had been declared between Great Britain and Germany. *Erin*'s master then contacted a British cruiser in the vicinity and was ordered to make for Bermuda. After spending a few days there she completed her voyage to New York and then returned to a British port, to be placed by Lipton at the disposal of the Red Cross. Soon the Duchess of Westminster was sailing in *Erin* to France with a number of doctors, nursing sisters and orderlies, plus medical stores and equipment, only to be somewhat rebuffed by Lord Kitchener, who disliked amateur interference in soldiers' concerns. *Erin* thereupon took the Duchess to Serbia with a hospital unit; the yacht had now been painted in hospital ship colours with red crosses along her sides. In Piraeus the King and Queen of the Hellenes lunched on board, then photographs were taken of the King and Queen, Prince George and Prince Alexander of Greece, Prince Henry of Battenberg, and the Grand Duchess George of Russia. In Yugoslavia soon after, from the royal palace balcony, Lipton saw Belgrade being shelled by the Austrian armies, an intense artillery bombardment which he watched at a discreet distance. However, the Lipton name was both magic and news, and in America the press announced in large letters LIPTON UNDER FIRE. Tea had made it again.

Later in the war the great yacht was handed over for naval service, under her original name of *Aegusa*. In 1915 she was sunk in the Mediterranean when going to the assistance of a torpedoed warship and many of her crew were drowned. After the war Lipton replaced her with *Albion*, a steam yacht which, once again, he renamed *Erin*. A year before he died at the age of 83 Sir Thomas achieved one of his great ambitions: he was finally admitted to membership of the Royal Yacht Squadron.

OPPOSITE The fourth of the great *Meteors*, pride of Kaiser Wilhelm II, racing at the Kiel Regatta of 1909.

The proliferating Vanderbilts

There were literally dozens of Van der Bilts, Van Derbilts and latterly Vanderbilts, the first of them – Jan Aertson Van der Bilt – arriving in America from Holland as far back as 1640. Although poor at first, they did not remain so: they were hard workers in a country of opportunity and expansion, and were also men (and women) of acumen in business and social matters. The great-great-grandson of Jan Aertson was the practical sailor and shipowner, Corneel (Cornelius) Vanderbilt, who became famous world-wide as 'The Commodore', the richest man in the world.

The foundations of the Vanderbilt fortune were laid in 1810 by Corneel, The Commodore. He borrowed $100 from his mother at the age of 17, and bought a small boat known as a *periauger* to act as a general carrier around Upper New York Bay. In due course Corneel became not only a professional seaman of repute but also the owner of a fleet of coasting schooners and eventually of steamers. In 1854, with a capital of $11,000,000 and an annual income not far short of $3,000,000, Corneel made a 15,000-mile European trip in one of his own company's ships, the brand-new 270-ft brigantine-rigged paddler *North Star*. Built by Jeremiah Simonson of New York at a cost of around £100,000, she was a superb ship. Inside she was fitted out with rosewood furniture, a stove to heat the ten staterooms, marble and granite in the great dining saloon, and opulence throughout. The staterooms each had their own colour schemes and were heavily draped in silk hangings, with lace curtains around the beds.

Corneel sailed to the Baltic, to France and the Mediterranean and into Russian waters, taking with him his ten children and assorted in-laws, his own physician, a ship's purser who had previously run a restaurant, and a Baptist minister. These and a large crew were under the command of Captain Asa Eldridge. The fo'c'sle hands were all young-men-about-New York, signed on in the hope that some of the ship's glory would rub off on them. Five hundred of Corneel's friends and associates were aboard on her preliminary run from New York to Sandy Hook; from there the Vanderbilts sailed for Southampton and travelled on to London, where they were unkindly snubbed by the court and aristocracy. They had a better deal in Russia, where they met many of the Russian imperial family, before going on to Italy and Constantinople.

William Kissam Vanderbilt, nephew of the Commodore, took delivery of his first yacht in 1887, and named her *Alva* after his wife. She was a three-masted topsail schooner with engines capable of 12 knots at cruising speed. Many of the fittings were of teak, with teak and mahogany panelling. On the main deck were the chartroom and galley, and a reception lounge from which a grand staircase led to a lower lobby, opening into the dining-room and Vanderbilt's own suite – no less than nine compartments plus a children's nursery. The saloon, decorated in gold-trimmed white enamel, measured 32 ft by 18 ft, with a nine-ft clearance to the deckhead; wood could be burned in its magnificent fireplace, and the furniture included a large central table, a fine sideboard and a grand piano. The room was lit at night by chandeliers, and fresh air could be admitted

OPPOSITE *Christina*, the 1,600-ton steam yacht owned by Aristotle Onassis. Her re-fitting in 1954 made her exceptionally elegant and luxurious; she was the focus of an élite social life and a colossal business empire.

RIGHT A stateroom aboard *Erin*.

BELOW *Erin*'s saloon, comparable with the most sumptuous drawing-rooms of the era.

through a large sliding skylight. Other apartments included a walnut-panelled library, also with a fireplace and skylight. Over the boiler-room was a comfortable settee for Vanderbilt's guests to watch the labours of the black gang as they toiled at the engines below.

Each of the seven staterooms had its own bathroom, in those days a luxury indeed: *Alva*, whose building had cost about $500,000, was said to be the world's most expensive yacht of the time. There were 53 in the crew, including a master, two mates, a surgeon, 24 seamen, a carpenter, a chief engineer and two assistants, 13 engine-room hands, an electrician, a chief steward, two under-stewards, three cooks – and even a refrigeration engineer, the very first of the species.

The ship's first cruise was to the West Indies and Vanderbilt embarked with his family, his children's governess and his wife's maid. Next, *Alva* cruised to Europe, Turkey and Egypt, during which trip the crew struck (or mutinied, strictly speaking) for more pay; whereupon Vanderbilt sacked all the strikers and cruised on with a depleted complement. It was during this cruise that Vanderbilt's wife Alva cast fond eyes upon one of her guests, O. H. P. Belmont, the H. prophetically standing for Hazard. Oliver Hazard Perry Belmont was a most attractive bachelor and the Vanderbilt divorce took place in March 1895, a Miss Nellie Neustretter from Eureka acting as official co-respondent.

Cornelius Vanderbilt III owned the steam yacht *North Star*, a fabulous vessel 233 ft in length, named after the steamer that had belonged to his great-great-grandfather the Commodore. By Vanderbilt standards, this Cornelius was not supremely rich, merely comfortable on $7,000,000. The expenses of such a large vessel were something of a strain, though the finances stretched to the provision of uniforms for his children, complete with naval-style cap ribbons proclaiming SY *North Star*. Cruising on one occasion to Naples, the family met Edward VII who invited them on board his own yacht; then on to Germany where they met Kaiser Wilhelm II, so soon to be at war with their previous host; and finally to Russia where they were entertained by Tsar Nicholas II. The outbreak of the First World War found Cornelius aboard *North Star* off Le Havre, from whence his financial manœuvrings and his urgent trips to London, Paris and Switzerland were said to have lifted the exchange rates in favour of the dollar. After this, he generously passed *North Star* over to Britain to be used as a hospital ship.

Many of the Vanderbilts took a great interest in sailing yachts: in 1893 William Kissam's *Defender* beat the British entry *Valkyrie III* in the America's Cup; in 1903 Cornelius III's syndicate, defending with *Reliance*, beat the British challenger, Lipton's *Shamrock III*. Later, in 1934, Harold Vanderbilt skippered *Rainbow*, and was that year's winner against *Endeavour*.

William Kissam II, who also took a keen interest in sailing, owned the steam yacht *Tarantula* in the first decade of the twentieth century. Renamed *Tuna*, sadly she was sunk whilst in service with the Royal Canadian Navy during the First World War; after the war Vanderbilt took over an auxiliary schooner, *Genesee*, in which he cruised the West Indies. In 1921 he bought a small French vessel which had seen war service – the

RIGHT Autumn 1914. Sir
Thomas Lipton surrounded by
nurses when *Erin* took a
hospital unit to Serbia.

BELOW *Erin* as a hospital
ship in the service of the Red
Cross.

870-ton motor yacht *Ara* of three decks, 213 ft in length, with a range of 10,000 miles. After re-engining her and improving her accommodation, he visited Scotland for the shooting and then sailed to North Africa before returning home via Miami. On the next cruise, a specimen-collecting trip to the Caribbean, the yacht's quartermaster, a Swede, attempted to jettison the officers over the side, a task from which he was dissuaded; he was subsequently put in gaol. Meanwhile William Kissam had formed an alliance with Mrs Rosamund Warburton – and two more marriages were set for disaster.

Romance, however, was not all along divorce lines: in 1895, William Kissam Vanderbilt's yacht *Valiant* helped along the marriage between his daughter Consuelo and the young Duke of Marlborough, uncle of Sir Winston Churchill; while across the seas in Cowes, the yachting scene, with no Vanderbilts involved on this occasion, formed the backdrop to the courting of Jenny Jerome of America and Lord Randolph Churchill, parents of Sir Winston.

In 1931 a second *Alva* replaced *Ara*. The new *Alva* was the last word, even for a man who had everything: in addition to the now customary staterooms, each with a bath, she carried a seaplane, a gymnasium, a rowing machine, a mechanical horse to shake up the overfed livers, four lifeboats – and a power launch for transport between ship and shore for late-night parties in harbour. The rich lived well.

The Astors

The Astors were a family formidable in both wealth and numbers, who, like the Vanderbilts, exerted their influence over the political scene in both America and Britain. John Jacob Astor, like King Henry, was eighth of his line in just one branch of this remarkable family tree. It was, however, William Backhouse Astor Junior who was the great yachting man of his times, owning the sailing yacht *Ambassadress* and later the *Nourmahal*, or 'Light of the Harem', one of the giants of the day. William Astor made frequent use of these vessels, largely as a means of avoiding his wife Caroline, who enjoyed the pleasures of New York society more than those of the sea – or William; the feeling in fact was mutual.

William Astor often rode at anchor off Florida, and he it was who founded the Florida Yacht Club, becoming its first Commodore. His son, John Jacob IV, was not quite the sailor his father had been, and, whilst piloting *Nourmahal*, had many collisions, not only with moving vessels but also with piers and wharfs. He was sued by the Vanderbilts for $15,000 damages after colliding with their yacht *North Star*. John Jacob, however, like all the Astors, was a man of money; the damages paid, he proceeded to an expensive refit of *Nourmahal* during which he increased the seating in his dining saloon to a round 60. For no apparent reason, except that he had a phobia about being attacked by pirates, he mounted four guns in a deck battery; the guns, however, failed to avert disaster, which came not long after the refit when *Nourmahal* was piled up on some rocks.

A later *Nourmahal* was sailed by the eccentric practical joker William Vincent Astor in the twenties and thirties; President Roosevelt was a

ABOVE Cornelius Vanderbilt's paddle yacht *North Star*, a luxurious brigantine-rigged vessel which cost him around £100,000 in 1854. BELOW Cornelius Vanderbilt, 'the richest man in the world' in his day and known as 'The Commodore'. BELOW RIGHT Two more Vanderbilts, both William Kissam Vanderbilt, grandson and great-grandson of the Commodore.

frequent guest aboard, Astor having built a ramp for the easier access of Roosevelt's wheel-chair. This *Nourmahal*, built in Germany by Krupp to the design of the American Cox and Stevens, was of almost 2,000 tons, with a 264-ft length. Fast and powerful, she was said to have cost Astor something like a million dollars, which sum was partly offset by the sale of the previous vessel – one of whose potential purchasers agreed to buy the yacht only if Astor would in return buy his orang-utang, Freda.

The new *Nourmahal* was splendid: a three-decker, she boasted a library panelled in pine, comfortable, ornate lounges, a dining saloon panelled in walnut, and even an operating theatre for emergency use. There were eight staterooms for guests, each with private bath, plus opulent rooms for the Astors themselves. The crew numbered 42, and the owner's eccentricity extended even to the provision of gun-mountings for his self-defence in time of war. The cost of maintaining all this was put at some $125,000 a year.

William Vincent Astor's extraordinarily inventive mind led him to the perpetration of cruel practical jokes, one of which at least centred upon *Nourmahal*: a guest, a wealthy businessman, became increasingly distraught as a result of daily wireless reports indicating the complete collapse of his financial empire on the New York Stock Exchange. In a state of frenzy and near to suicide, he eventually disembarked, only to discover that it had all been a leg-pull, Astor having made himself fully acquainted in advance with his guest's financial holdings so as to lend an air of total authenticity to the trick.

In February 1932 President-elect Roosevelt was aboard *Nourmahal* for a ten-day cruise that took in Miami; throughout he was in touch with Washington by the yacht's radio – indeed he did much of his cabinet-making from *Nourmahal*'s comfort and seclusion. During the yacht's stay in Miami a man named Giuseppe Zangara attempted to assassinate Roosevelt: a fusillade of shots was fired at the President-elect's car, killing the Mayor of Chicago, Anton Cermac, and wounding some of the onlookers.

Lucy Kavaler, in her book *The Astors*, describes how William Vincent Astor, during a cruise off the Latin American coast, asked if he could accompany one of that continent's emergent dictators on a shark-fishing expedition. As they were about to start, a horse was brought on deck by a party of soldiers, and when the vessel was well into shark territory the wretched horse was pushed over the side. The soldiers opened fire on it as it struggled in the water, the blood then attracting the sharks which were shot in their turn. A drunken brawl ensued, and on approaching the shore on the return trip, the dictator ordered one of his ministers to strip and dive in; the unfortunate man did as he was told, and was propelled the faster inshore by the guns of the party on deck.

William Vincent Astor, eccentric or not, was a whole-hearted lover of life at sea. He took a great interest in naval affairs world-wide, and spent much time cruising the world, not simply for the pleasure it gave him, but often in the interests of science as well. He frequently included botanists and ornithologists on his guest list, and the yacht would return home carrying unusual specimens, such as exotic fish caught off the Galapagos

Islands, strange cacti, and rare sea plants from Fiji. He also hunted for lost treasure in the Cocos Islands – unsuccessfully as it turned out.

When war came in 1939 William Vincent presented *Nourmahal* to the United States Navy and he himself became a Captain in the USNR and a commodore of convoys. Some years after the war President Truman was advised to accept *Nourmahal* as his Presidential yacht in place of *Potomac*; but Truman refused on the ground that *Nourmahal* was too big for use by the President of the United States.

John Pierpont Morgan

J. P. Morgan was the owner of a succession of *Corsairs* – I, II, III, and IV. A gigantic fortune inherited from his father, together with his own banking and shipping interests, enabled him to indulge his hobby to the full. The Steel Trust, which he piloted into being in 1901, had a capital of around $1,500,000,000 and Morgan became the world's most powerful single financial force. His *Corsairs* were the backdrop to many of his dealings, notably when he brought aboard Chauncy Depew, politician and president of the New York Central Railroad Company, in July 1885. Here, free from telephones and other interruption – and also with a guest who couldn't disembark without Morgan's agreement – certain highly important railroad amalgamations were agreed.

Corsair III, a twin-screw, steel-built schooner with two masts and a single funnel, came from the yard of T. S. Marvel of Newburgh, New York, and was designed by J. Beavor Webb. Launched in 1899, she carried all the usual and expected fittings of luxury: deck lounges, a domed dining saloon, a library and six staterooms, plus cabins for the professional officers. The crew included ladies' maids and valets. Even the engine-room was a place of some splendour, the cylinders being encased in highly polished maple. Of 1,396 tons, she was 304 ft in length with a beam of 33.5 ft, and could steam at 19 knots. She was to be followed by *Corsair IV* in 1930. At 2,142 tons and a 343-ft length, she was then the largest yacht to have been built for private service, but was overtaken within a year by *Savarona*.

Other Private Cruisers

Savarona III, built in 1931, was owned by the American millionairess Mrs Emily Cadwalader, whose grandfather had built Brooklyn Bridge. This gigantic yacht, of 4,677 tons, was designed by Gibbs and Cox of New York but built in Hamburg by Bloehm and Voss. With a length of 408 ft and a 53-ft beam, she carried a massive crew of 107. Something of a tax-avoidance venture, she kept well clear of US waters once she was in commission. She was a superb creation, the largest private yacht in the world and beautifully proportioned; she had two raked masts, a long bowsprit over a clipper bow, two squat funnels and a capability of 21 knots. In size she was approached only by J. P. Morgan's *Corsair IV*, designed by H. J. Gielow.

In 1938 the great *Savarona* passed to the Turks, first as the presidential

RIGHT John Pierpont Morgan, financier extraordinary with a great love of the sea.

BELOW *Corsair II*, one of J. P. Morgan's superb steam yachts and a vessel of great beauty.

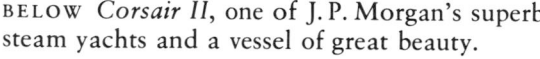

yacht – thus the biggest state yacht after the *Victoria and Albert* – and later as a training ship for the Turkish Navy.

In 1888 Fairfield's of Govan built the steam yacht *Lady Torfreda* of 735 tons, a 216-ft two-deck screw-schooner with electric lighting. Her first owner was Sir William Pearce, but later she was sold to the American millionaire Bayard Brown, who renamed her *Valfreyia* and kept her moored off Brightlingsea in Essex from 1890 to 1927. For all that time her captain and full crew were ready and waiting, and steam was always on the boilers. Bayard Brown was accustomed on occasion to turn the hoses on his crew, and to put pep in their step by firing off a revolver behind them. No maintenance was done to the yacht and she began to crumble away, being unfit to be taken into naval service when war broke out in 1914. After the war she was moved into dry dock for essential repairs, and there she remained for several years. The eccentric Bayard Brown, who certainly had the cash to meet the bills, nevertheless refused to leave the dock. In 1927 he was found dead aboard his yacht. Later she passed to the ownership of the Maharajah of Nawanagar – the cricketer Ranjit Singh – and thence to Lord Portal.

The auxiliary schooner *Ailée* was built in 1928 for Madame Virginie Heriot, a Frenchwoman well known in the racing of the 6-metre class yachts. *Ailée* was a three-master of 486 tons and passed eventually to the Naval Academy at Brest.

One of the last British auxiliary schooners to be built was *Sonia II* in 1931. Built of steel like *Ailée*, she was of 450 tons and a very beautiful vessel; the intention of her owner, Mrs Betty Carstairs, was to send her cruising the oceans and, like William Vincent Astor, to seek for treasure in the Cocos. On one occasion there was a race between *Ailée* and *Sonia II*, from the pierhead at Ryde in the Isle of Wight to Le Havre. Sir Malcolm Campbell was a guest aboard *Sonia II*, but despite his presence, it was *Ailée* who came home the winner.

The twin-screw steam yacht *Nahlin* was built on the Clyde in 1930 by John Brown and designed by G. L. Watson (it was to be his last steam yacht) for Lady Yule. She was of 1,574 tons, 250 ft long and capable of 17 knots. Her interior fittings were as opulent as anything that had gone before: three decks containing the owner's suite, six staterooms for guests, a gymnasium, a dining saloon and a drawing-room. A library stood aft on the awning deck, while forward a ladies' lounge had wide views of the sea. Her chief claim to fame rests upon Edward VIII's Mediterranean cruise in her during his brief reign in 1936, together with Mrs Wallis Simpson who was awaiting her divorce. The King chose *Nahlin* in preference to the royal yacht for this cruise. In the guise of Duke of Lancaster he embarked in Yugoslavia and thence, under escort by the destroyers *Grafton* and *Glowworm*, sailed to Greece and Turkey; among his guests were Duff Cooper, the British Minister of War, his wife Lady Diana and Lord and Lady Louis Mountbatten. During this cruise – the King happy and relaxed throughout – Mrs Simpson bought him a pair of swimming trunks in an isolated village, and a roving photographer caught the couple holding hands – a bonanza for the press. The King visited Turkey by request of the Foreign Office, a commercial treaty having just been signed between

RIGHT Edward VIII and Mrs Simpson in a dinghy at the stern of *Nahlin* in Novigrad Bay, Jugoslavia, during their Mediterranean cruise of 1936.

BELOW Night at sea, the darkness romantically lit by Chinese lanterns.

the two countries. Here Edward met the dictator, Kemal Atatürk; this was the first visit to Turkey from a powerful monarch since Kaiser Wilhelm II's, and was said to have had a beneficial effect on the line up of alliances in the coming war.

In the Adriatic *Nahlin* entered the Bocche di Cattaro, where a small town nestled below great walls; here the fortress guns fired a salute and the King's piper marched the yacht's decks playing *Over the Sea to Skye*, which Mrs Simpson found moving. And so *Nahlin* cruised on, the magic of the moon over dark waters no doubt helping the romance that was soon to deprive England of her monarch. In 1937 *Nahlin* passed to the government of Romania for use as a royal yacht; later she became a cruise ship.

The vast and impressive screw schooner *Rover* was built in 1930, the same year as *Nahlin*, for Lord Inchcape by Alexander Stephen. She was of 2,115 tons, with a length of 265 ft and a speed of nearly 16 knots; equipped with forced-draught ventilation, she was said to have been the best-equipped as well as the largest steam yacht ever built in Britain for private ownership. Together with *Nahlin* and *Xarifa*, built for F. M. Singer by Samuel White of Cowes and designed by J. M. Soper, *Rover* was the last of the British-built steam yachts before steam gave way to motor propulsion. *Rover* passed into the ownership of Axel Wenner-Genn, a Swede, before the outbreak of the Second World War, with her name changed to *Southern Cross*. In the first month of war she picked up a number of survivors from the torpedoed liner *Athenia*, which was crossing the North Atlantic carrying mainly women and children.

The life aboard and the crews

The big steam yachts were hotels afloat; most of them had central staircases like a smart London hotel or a transatlantic liner, with service to match. It was a life of splendour, sometimes of splendour-run-mad, always at an astronomical cost – and a life that was virtually over by 1939. These great vessels would sometimes lie off in the Thames – *Rover* was the last to do so, close by London Bridge in the thirties – and wild parties would be held, with expensively-clad guests arriving in taxis and taken off by cutters or power-boats for a taste of the high life with a difference – while strings of laden barges passed by, carrying their workaday cargoes.

Nights at sea were fantastic: one wealthy owner was reputed to have a sliding bulkhead between his stateroom and the adjoining one, and having made his selection from a bevy of beauties would allocate the lady of his choice to this contiguous berth. In the middle of the night he would operate his satanic mechanism and the lady would suddenly find herself, willy-nilly, in bed next to the owner. Nevertheless, there was as ever the other side of the picture: a long cruise could become incredibly boring if the company was not right, in spite of the pampered luxury and the continual supply of food and drink.

The crews of the British luxury yachts were professional seamen, some from the Merchant Service, some from the Royal Navy, others from fishing boats and coastal areas around the Thames estuary, the Solent and the

OPPOSITE, ABOVE Aristotle Onassis, Greek multi-millionaire, and his great steam yacht *Christina*, formerly a frigate of the Royal Canadian Navy.

OPPOSITE, BELOW President Franklin D. Roosevelt (far right) sailing with his children on Passamaquaddy Bay, New Brunswick.

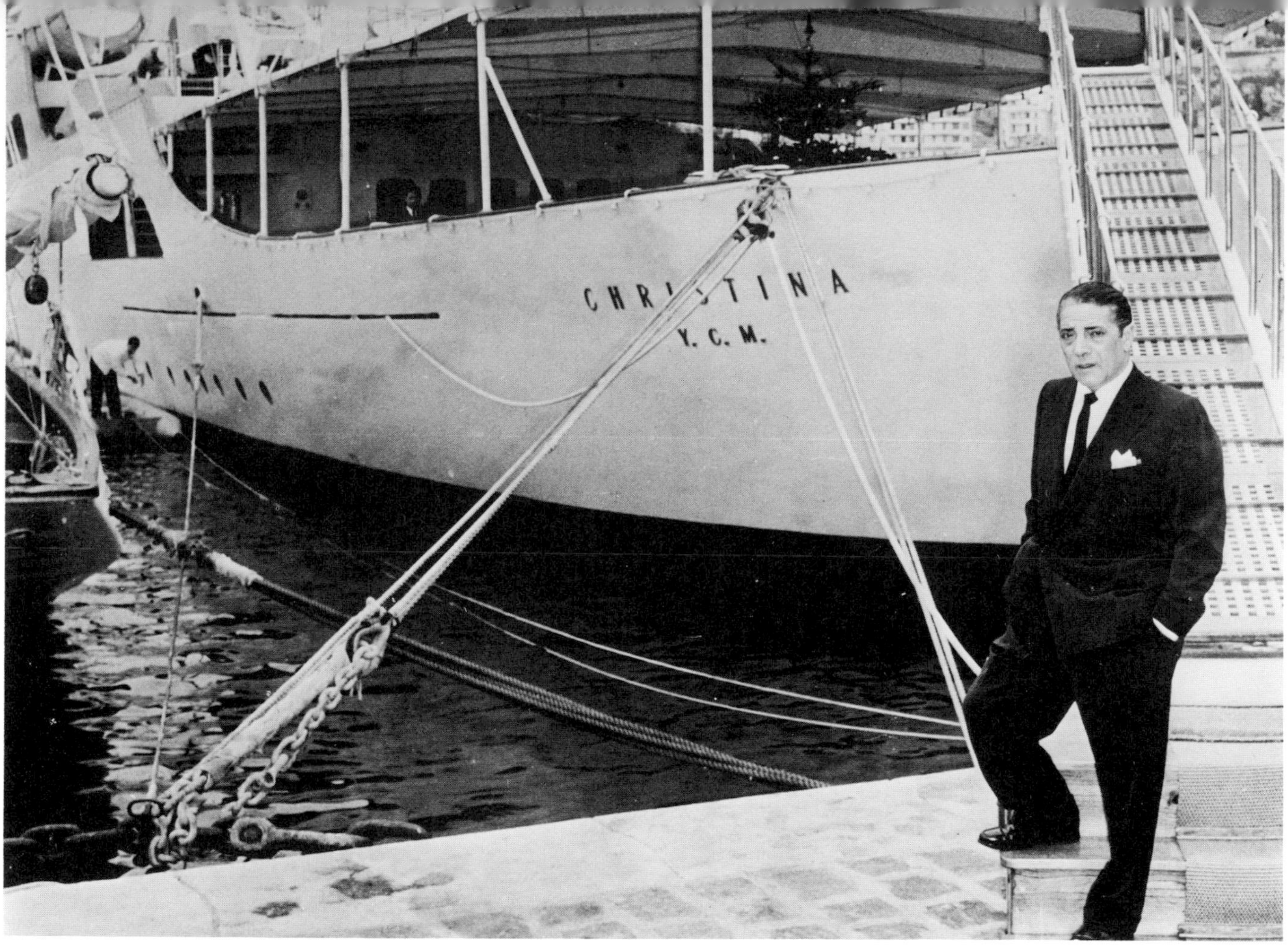
CHRISTINA
Y.C.M.

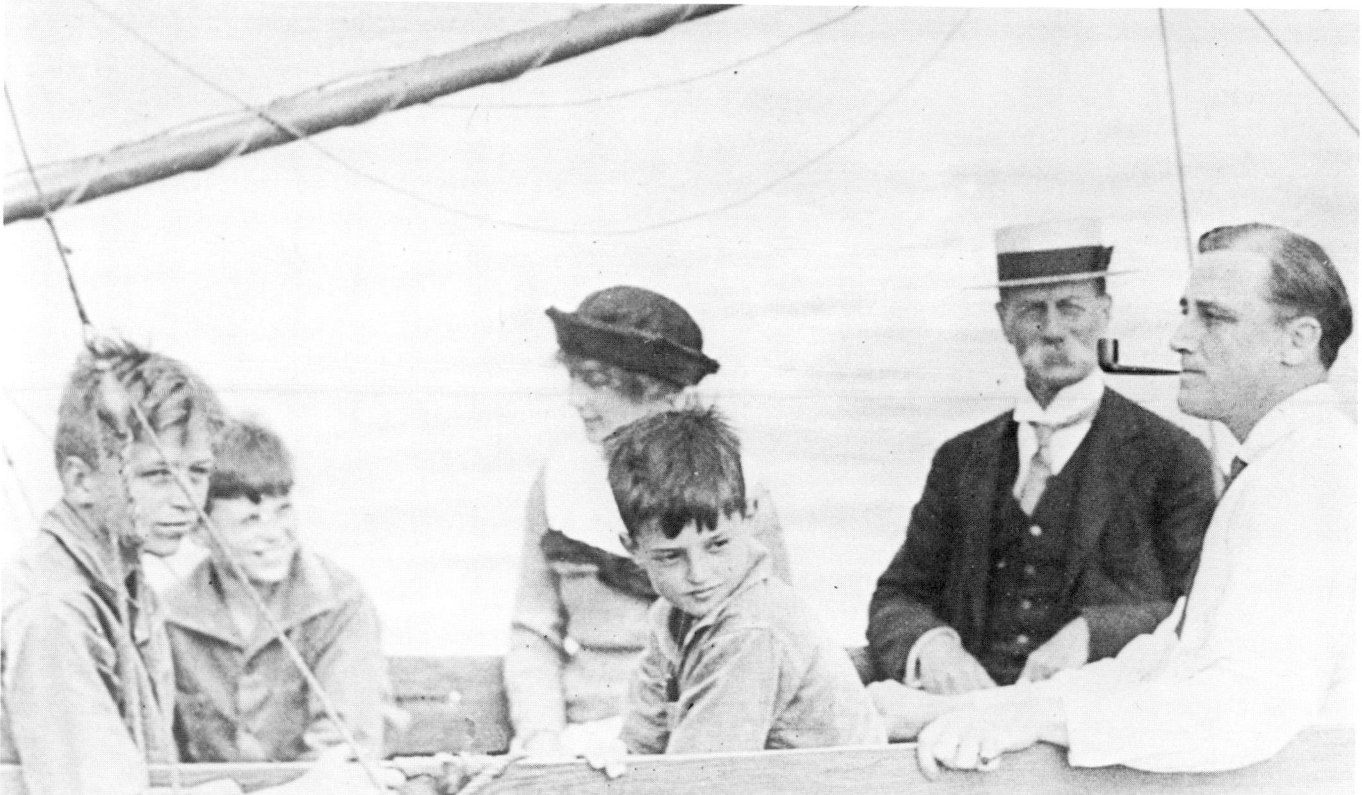

Clyde. Many of the masters had full Board of Trade foreign-going certificates of competency, and all would have had at least a yachtmaster's certificate. Their responsibilities were many: they had not only to navigate and shipkeep but also to deal with all the many port requirements and to manage stores and other cash deals, including payment of the crew. They suffered numerous disadvantages, for officially private yachts were neither fish, fowl nor good red herring; their status was nebulous and hard to define. Board of Trade backing was not automatic, for instance, in crew disputes, while the disastrous effects of an incompetent owner trying out his hand at ship-handling or navigation were always a possibility. If the worst happened a master stood fair to lose his certificate, forced as he was to accept his owner's whims and fancies, for in some yachts the owner was ever at the master's back, sometimes overruling him. In fact, he had to cope with a situation which cannot arise aboard a merchant ship, where the owner has no right of interference but is bound by law to leave the conduct of the ship at sea to the master, to whom the vessel is legally delivered once the Articles of Agreement have been signed – be it the *Queen Elizabeth* or a humble coaster.

The grandeur that still lives

Great private yachts now belong to the romantic past; in the post-war years money has run out for all except a handful of exceedingly rich men.

Aristotle Socrates Onassis, Greek multi-millionaire and shipowner – to the tune of around three million tons – who launched at least one of his fleet with holy water from Zem Zem's renowned fountain near Mecca, used to spend four or five months of each year aboard his splendid steam yacht *Christina*, the expensive apple of his eye, and largely regarded as his real home. Aboard, he was attended by a crew of 50 seamen, engineers and stewards, two ladies' maids, a butler and several valets, all commanded by a master mariner. Among his many guests have been bankers, oil company chiefs, tobacco and insurance magnates – rich men all but none so rich as Onassis.

Christina began her life as a frigate of the Royal Canadian Navy, but was bought by Onassis along with nine others for presentation to the Greek Government; however, the latter indulged in too much politicking for Onassis, who cancelled the whole scheme, sold off eight of the frigates, and retained *Stormont* (as she was then named) for his personal use; in 1954 she was converted to luxury at Kiel in Germany. The 1,600-ton *Christina* was perhaps the ultimate in yacht splendour, complete with a swimming-pool, a fully-equipped hospital, her own five-seater amphibious aircraft and no less than eight power boats for shore service. Onassis' own quarters consisted of three rooms: a study, a bedroom and a bathroom. The hardwood-panelled study reflected his interests: shipping, Greek and English classics, the arts, and the works of Sir Winston Churchill whom he so much admired. Over his desk hung El Greco's *Madonna and Angel*. The bedroom contained gold-plated toilet accessories and hairbrushes, the bathroom, lined with brown Siena marble, held a bath which was the replica of that used by King Minos of Crete in his Palace of Knossos; and

RIGHT Sir Bernard and Lady Docker in Monaco, aboard their diesel yacht *Shemara*.

BELOW *Shemara*, a neat, compact vessel. She passed after war service to the financier Harry Hyams.

even in there was a telephone extension (one of 40) so that Onassis could always keep in touch with his world-wide business and social interests: for *Christina* was virtually the heart of an empire.

The main saloon also did duty as a cinema, while aft was a splendid smoking-room which had a fireplace made from lapis lazuli, an elegant blue edifice said to have been put in at a cost of some four dollars per square inch. In the adjoining bar the stools were covered with leather made from the testicles of whales; the bulkheads were lined with maps and miniature models of vessels famous in history. Every conceivable drink, borne to the guests by a butler, was available. Guest accommodation was provided in nine double cabins complete with baths and showers, lavatories, washbasins and bidets, all in a variety of coloured marbles.

Aboard the yacht Onassis carried a figure of Buddha, carved in jade embedded with diamonds and rubies, its tongue wagging to the yacht's movements at sea; it is one of only two such figures, the other being the property of the British Queen.

Christina's hull, white-painted, below a single large buff funnel, shows the yacht's warship origins: the lines are there still, only the rebuilt upperworks indicating the pleasure purpose that succeeded war's austerity. But *Christina* was not always bent purely on pleasure: in July 1956 she was bound for the Aegean when an earthquake occurred on the island of Santorini; the city of Thera was being destroyed and the cathedral was already shattered. Onassis came swiftly to the rescue of the inhabitants, altering course for Piraeus and organizing the provision of food and medical equipment from Athens. These he took aboard and the *Christina* sailed for the disaster area, the swimming-pool filled with fresh water; Onassis's wife Tina saw to the allocation of the food and stores.

Christina's cruises were many and varied: all over the Mediterranean – Asia Minor, Crete, Monte Carlo, Sardinia, Spain, Venice, the Dardanelles – Saudi Arabia, the Canary Islands, New York, Nassau, Argentina (where her owner, ashore, was mistaken for an American gangster), with Onassis constantly in touch by radio with his business interests. Among his cruise guests when he sailed to the Dardanelles was Sir Winston Churchill, who revisited the military graves of Gallipoli where so many men from Britain and the Empire had died. Other guests from time to time included Prince and Princess Rainier of Monaco – on one occasion whilst a film unit from Hollywood was embarked, Onassis asked Grace Kelly if she too was connected with the film industry – Greto Garbo, the Begum Aga Khan, the Earl of Warwick, the Maharajah of Baroda, the Guinnesses, Dame Margot Fonteyn, ex-King Peter of Yugoslavia, ex-King Farouk of Egypt, Lady Docker – and Jackie Kennedy. Possibly his favourite apart from Jackie was Sir Winston Churchill; it is said that when Churchill repaid some hospitality by asking Onassis to dine with him at Marrakesh in Morocco, it cost Onassis five thousand dollars to arrive for the meal – but this was aboard a DC-6 and not *Christina*. When Churchill became too old to negotiate the accommodation ladder, Onassis arranged for the ladder to be pulled up with him on it. Onassis, in spite of the splendour of his yacht and the complexity of his business life, was an unassuming

OPPOSITE The royal steam yacht *Britannia*, largest of the world's state yachts, at the RTYC Bicentenary Regatta at Cowes. The pennant of the club's patron, HRH the Duke of Edinburgh, flies from her mizzen mast.

Albemarle
1930 Before Alterations
On Britannia

Sir Philip Hunloke GCVO.

and unobtrusive man, and surprisingly humble: he was overawed by the fame of Churchill, and delighted by his friendship.

The decisions he made whilst afloat affected the employment of many thousands of men and women and their families. *Christina*'s radio was a much-used link: through it went orders for ships, credits, a $30,000,000 action against a fellow shipowner (decided while Onassis cruised happily in the Caribbean), decisions vitally affecting his Middle Eastern oil interests and his interests in the tourist trade in Greece, where a military coup had taken place.

On 12 April 1956, *Christina* fired off a barrage of fireworks in Monte Carlo harbour to welcome Grace Kelly when she arrived to marry Prince Rainier. In front of a huge crowd the yacht gave the best firework display ever seen on the Riviera. It was after this, while *Christina* was off Venice's Grand Canal the following year, that Onassis first met Maria Callas who was to become his close friend and companion, and whose break with her husband eventually came about during a cruise with Onassis in *Christina*.

There was much rivalry between Onassis and Niarchos, another million-aire shipowner from Greece, not least as to their yachts. *Christina* was beautiful and very large, but Niarchos's 190-ft *Creole*, though smaller, was perhaps the more eye-catching: a three-masted schooner with a black painted hull, a sailing vessel rather than a steam yacht, she made a very graceful sight. *Creole* was the biggest ship under sail in private hands (with a total sail area of 8,555 sq ft), and her saloon was decorated with murals by Salvador Dali, who was said to have been paid $250,000 for his pains. The crew numbered 32 under a master, but Niarchos did a great deal of the ship's handling himself, and has entered some of the international ship races under his own helmsmanship. Members of the Greek royal family were often entertained aboard before the military coup in 1967 which deprived King Paul and Queen Frederica of their throne; Niarchos was more inclined than Onassis to prefer upper class personages to inter-national tycoonery. An art lover, he fitted out a special saloon for the dis-play of a number of valuable painting acquisitions – Cézannes, Gauguins, Renoirs, Degas and van Goghs among them, as well as works by Toulouse-Lautrec, El Greco, Goya and Matisse. To preserve them the room was air-conditioned so that humidity and temperature were controlled, and all cigarette smoke was expelled by means of an extractor. Niarchos was accustomed to spend almost half of each year aboard *Creole*, mainly cruis-ing in the Mediterranean.

Shemara, 878 tons, was built in 1938 by Thornycroft for Sir Bernard and Lady Docker of gold-starred Daimler fame. A frequent visitor to Monte Carlo in pre-war days, she was a diesel yacht with twin screws, 212 ft in length with a 30-ft beam and a 13-ft draught. She was a good-looking two-master with a single squat funnel, her symmetrical lines and straight sheer – the upward slope of her hull towards the bow and stern – giving her a deserved look of speed, for she was capable of 16 knots. Life aboard was comfortable for the crew as well as the guests: the Dockers

OPPOSITE Major Sir Philip Hunloke, George V's sailing master and a well-known and intrepid yachtsman, at the helm of *Britannia*.

were good employers who made no deduction for food from the crew's wages – unusual in those pre-war days. She carried a professional chef, but apart from the cruises to Monte Carlo his services were not needed for long; at the outbreak of war, *Shemara* passed into naval service to be used at Portland and Campbeltown for anti-submarine training. In 1968 she was bought from the Dockers by Harry Hyams, the British financier.

Sir Thomas Sopwith's *Philante*, of 1,629 tons, was the biggest motor yacht from a British yard – Camper and Nicholson built her in 1937. Sopwith's last yacht, she was magnificently fitted out, her three decks including a sun deck and accommodation for as many as 18 seamen, cabins for 16 officers and stewards, and the owner's suite. There were five saloons for different functions; the dining saloon, 20 by 30 ft, was decorated in the Adam style and fitted with French windows at each end; the accommodation and alleys were panelled in oak and walnut, and the doors covered in leather. Her eight guest rooms were superbly furnished and had plenty of headroom. The yacht was equipped with a sickbay, storerooms (including a cold store) and an up-to-date galley fitted with a variety of stoves. Forerunner of what was to be the post-war style in motor yachts, *Philante* passed to Norway in 1947 to become King Haakon's royal yacht *Norge*; this was after war service with the Royal Navy during which she operated in many sectors; at the end of the war she acted as escort into Loch Eriboll for the surrendered German submarines.

In 1961 Camper and Nicholson's yard produced another motor yacht, the 109-ton *Philante V* (since renamed *Binta*) for Sopwith's son Thomas. Very well appointed, the new yacht, though small, was capable of 20 knots.

The royal yacht *Britannia* was built in 1954 by John Brown on Clydebank, to Admiralty specifications; of 5,111 tons, she has a length of 412 ft, a 55-ft beam and is capable of 22·75 knots; she is fitted with stabilizers. The biggest of all the world's state and royal yachts today, she steamed 90,000 miles in her first three years afloat and has taken members of the royal family to many parts of the world. With her single funnel and three nicely raked masts, her upperworks painted white and her steel hull dark blue, she is an imposing sight as she leaves her Portsmouth base on royal duty. She is engined by geared steam turbines with oil-fired water-tube boilers; the internal fittings bear comparison with the beautiful appointments of the old *Victoria and Albert* and the same 'quiet routine' is observed by her officers and ratings as was observed before the war. She is specifically constructed for quick and easy conversion to hospital ship duties in the event of war. Her visits to Cowes for the regatta week are not so frequent as were those of her various predecessors, but she has not wholly deserted the social scene. Her presence can be memorably impressive, especially when the Queen is embarked and *Britannia* wears the Royal Standard at the mainmast head, the flag of the Lord High Admiral at the fore, the Union Flag at the mizzen, and the White Ensign floating from the ensign staff aft.

RIGHT *Britannia*'s drawing-room, with Norman Wilkinson's painting of her launch in 1954.

BELOW The great royal yacht *Britannia*, the only ship of the Royal Navy to be commanded by a rear-admiral. She is shown leaving Suva in Fiji for New Zealand.

4 Great Ocean Racers

*I*n 1875 the Yacht Racing Association was formed under the presidency of the Marquis of Exeter, Commodore of the Isle of Wight's Royal Victoria Yacht Club. The YRA's object was to form a body with some control over design, and also to introduce penalties for designs that broke the rules already drawn up with the agreement of the yacht clubs, 35 of which were now represented on the committee. Since rules had the effect of changing rig, design and construction, the early measurement rules had produced deep draught vessels of small beam with extremely heavy keels to counterbalance the weight of canvas. Towards the end of the nineteenth century Dixon Kemp, an authority on yacht racing and secretary of the Yacht Racing Association, introduced the rating of yachts on their load-waterline length alone, plus sail area, beam being discounted. This led to much more seaworthy vessels with more beam, examples of this new construction being the cutters *Valkyrie* (Lord Dunraven) and *Iverna* (Jameson).

It was not until 1906 that the International Rules for measurement and classification came into being: the object of these new rules being the production of what one might perhaps call a composite of the two main types of yacht – the racing yacht and the cruising yacht, the former hitherto designed to give a maximum showing over set courses, the latter going for stability and comfort. Under the new rules the vessels were allocated to eleven classes, the biggest, Class A, being given the A1 classification at Lloyds of London. In addition to Lloyds, classifications were given by Norsk Veritas, Germanischer Lloyd and Bureau Veritas. Agreement on acceptance of the rules was wide and included all the European countries as well as the Argentine, Hungary and Russia, the United States of America being the only interested party to stand outside. For both cruising and racing the gaff-rigged cutter still prevailed in popularity. The weight of gear was still immense: masts of Oregon pine, long bowsprits, heavy ropes and wires and great sail areas.

By the end of the nineteenth century America was very well to the forefront of racing, thanks largely to the designs of the Herreshoff brothers and Edward Burgess, a naturalist turned yacht designer, producer of the compromise-design *Puritan* which beat the British challenger *Genesta* in the 1884 America's Cup races. *Puritan* subsequently had an enormous influence on both British and American designers, being less beamy than earlier racers but with more draught. In 1885 another Burgess-designed yacht, *Mayflower*, won against the British *Galatea*, and two years later his *Volunteer* beat the challenge of the Royal Clyde Yacht Club's entry *Thistle*, the yacht that was later to pass to the German Emperor.

Burgess had made a tremendous contribution to American yacht racing; in recognition of his great services a subscription was raised towards the end of his life and he was presented with a cheque for $10,000. His son Starling Burgess was to carry on the family name in yacht design, especially after the First World War; but the immediate mantle fell, when Edward Burgess died, on Herreshoff. Herreshoff designed the famed cutter *Gloriana* in 1891 to conform to the new 46-ft class under the Seawanhaka Rule; after sustaining a barrage of hostile and sceptical opinion, *Gloriana* sailed to a win in all of her eight first season races. In 1904 Herreshoff designed the schooner *Ingomar* for Morton A. Plant. *Ingomar* proved a real winner, taking many prizes in British and German waters.

The racing of large yachts was very much an occupation for the wealthy and indeed was to remain so: when the cash ran out, the yachts grew smaller. The operation of the Rules – one measurement formula for Britain, another for America – meant that yachts had to be designed and built purely for one series – the America's Cup, the winning of which had become a fetish with British owners – leaving the yacht concerned unable to race in British waters.

Tom Lipton was much in evidence on the yacht racing scene as the twentieth century got under way. In 1913, not long before the First World War put an end to that era, he brought out *Shamrock IV* as his fourth challenge for the America's Cup. Designed by Charles Nicholson to conform to the American rating rules, *Shamrock IV* had been cut to 75 ft on the waterline, 110 ft overall, including her overhangs fore and aft. She was of very light construction for a large racer, with three-skin side-planking of laminated cedar, spruce and mahogany, laminated wood timbers, and navaltum web frames. Not a pretty vessel, she was strong and stable and her building caused the Cup defenders to hasten forward three new possible challengers – though these efforts were interrupted by the outbreak of war. *Shamrock*, already at sea, continued on passage, to be laid up for the duration.

In 1920 Lipton re-issued his challenge and *Shamrock IV* was refitted. American honour was to be defended by *Resolute*, designed by Nat Herreshoff, and, being slightly the larger of the two, *Shamrock* had to concede some time allowance; the first race in the series took place over the Long Island Sound course in rain with plenty of wind. *Resolute* was well in the lead when she suffered the misfortune of breaking her main gaff. The defender was unable to finish and *Shamrock* was the winner, though, in a typically sportsmanlike gesture, Lipton was ready to give up the race in deference to the sheer bad luck befouling his opponent. However, Sherman Hoyt, that great American helmsman who was aboard *Resolute*

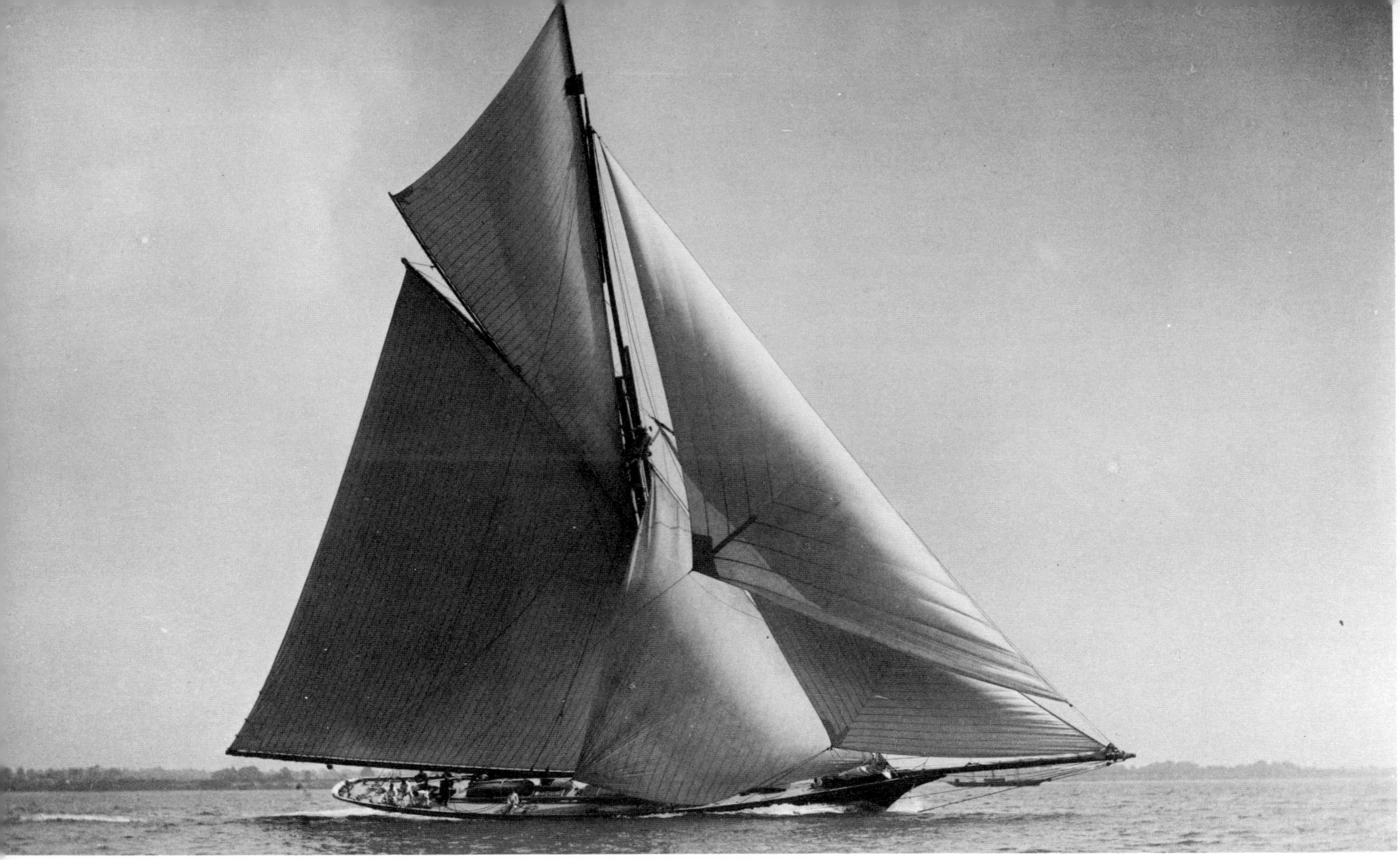

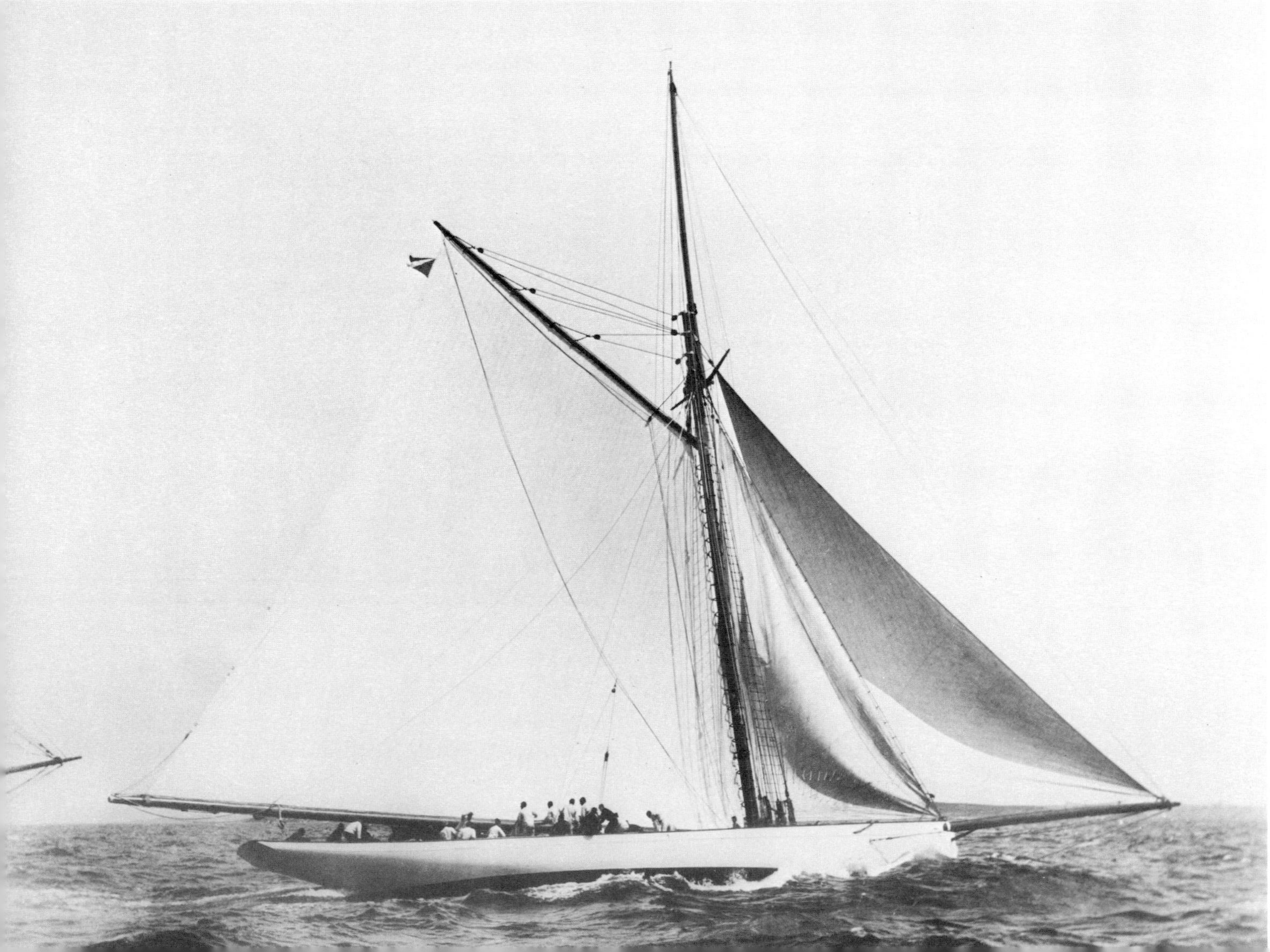

representing the New York Yacht Club, refused to accept the offer, his opinion being that racing must also test a vessel's gear.

In the second race Sir William Burton, Vice-President of the YRA, at *Shamrock*'s helm, went ahead of *Resolute*, steered by Charles Adams, US Secretary of the Navy, and started well away in patchy conditions that often dropped to a dead calm. *Shamrock* kept her initial lead and flew on to win by something over nine minutes, though in corrected time this great performance was scaled down to two-and-a-half minutes.

The third in the series showed the defender two minutes of elapsed (uncorrected) time ahead at the outer marker buoy; as each contender shook out their spinnakers *Shamrock* closed the gap and then began to move into the lead, and the defenders believed that the Cup really was about to go back to Britain. However, this was not to be; *Shamrock* crossed the line 19 seconds in the lead, but the necessary time allowance to the smaller boat deprived her of victory. With two to one in favour of Britain, the fourth race was to start in a stiff wind and sea running off Sandy Hook, but the committee decided on a deferment and then a cancellation. When the race did take place, *Resolute* had an easy win; while in the fifth, though *Shamrock* did well enough at the start, *Resolute* was once more the winner.

This series of the America's Cup races, the first since the war, was also the first in which the skippers were amateurs rather than professional sailors. In this new era, though the deckhands remained professional, it was the amateurs such as Sir Thomas Sopwith who began to take the helm personally, unlike Lipton who, not himself a sailor, handed command to Captain Duncan Neill. The series also proved to be the last in which gaff-rigged yachts took part. The Bermudian rig, more efficient in aerodynamic terms, was on the way in; *Nyria*, belonging to Mrs R. E. Workman and built back in 1906, was the first of the big cutters to shift to this rig.

The Fastnet race, now the oldest of all distance races in British waters, was first run in 1925. The course was from Ryde in the Isle of Wight to Plymouth and it was the competitors themselves who, after the race, instituted the Royal Ocean Racing Club, though at that time the appellation 'Royal' had not yet been granted. The inauguration of the RORC took place at the dinner held for the competitors at Plymouth's Royal Western Yacht Club when it was decided to make the race an annual event, though subsequently a decision was reached to alternate this event with the New York to Bermuda race. Soon after this the racing calendar began to expand: in 1928 the first Channel Race was run from Southsea to the Royal Sovereign Tower, on to Le Havre and back to Southsea, a distance of 225 miles; in 1929 the Plymouth to Santander; the Cowes to Dinard in 1930, the 180-mile course running from Cowes to the River Rance, for the King Edward VII Challenge Cup; and in 1931 the Round-the-Island (60 miles from Cowes to Cowes) for the Gold Roman Bowl.

The present-day course for the Fastnet, now part of the Admiral's Cup series, is from Cowes, round the Fastnet Lighthouse and the Scillies, finishing at Plymouth – a total run of 605 miles. The 1925 race attracted only seven starters, most of them converted from pilot cutters and other kinds

OPPOSITE, ABOVE Lord Dunraven's beautiful cutter *Valkyrie* in 1891. She was a well-known racer at Cowes and elsewhere.

OPPOSITE, BELOW The American sloop *Puritan*, designed by Edward Burgess, and winner of the 1884 America's Cup.

of working boats, all of them elderly; by 1973 this entry had grown to 258. One of the great names of the Fastnet race was the German *Nordwind* which held the course record from just before the Second World War until 1965, when Baron Edmund de Rothschild's *Gitana IV* took it from her; another and earlier one was *Jolie Brise*, a Le Havre pilot-boat that won the first race and was to win again in 1929 and 1930. She was owned by the first Commodore of the Royal Ocean Racing Club, Commander E. G. Martin.

The great J-class yachts made their debut in the 1930s. Vessels of between 80 and 90 feet on the waterline, they carried lofty spreads of canvas and were perhaps the most beautiful yachts to be seen at that time – perhaps never surpassed since in that respect. Intended mainly for the big-yacht racing scene at Cowes and also to carry on the challenge for the America's Cup (in 1930 Britain and America had adopted the Universal Rule for vessels larger than the $14\frac{1}{2}$-metre classes, so the old limitation no longer applied), they sadly did not succeed in the latter aim.

The first of the J-class was Lipton's *Shamrock V*, composite built, with mahogany planking and steel frames, constructed by Camper and Nicholson at Gosport in Hampshire. In 1930 she challenged for the America's Cup. America had had a difficult task in deciding who should have the honour of defence, the great *Weetamoe* being one of the yachts under consideration. *Weetamoe* was owned by the Morgan syndicate consisting of George Nichols, Cornelius Vanderbilt, J. P. Morgan, Arthur Curtiss James, George T. Bowdoin, Gerard Lambert and Henry Walters – a very wealthy and influential group of men. She had been built by Herreshoff and designed by Clinton Crane. Skippered by George Nichols with J. Christiansen as sailing master, she was a close contender but, along with *Whirlwind* and *Yankee* (which was to take part in George v's Silver Jubilee review of the Fleet at Spithead in 1935) and the modernized cutter *Vanity*, she was beaten in the final choice by *Enterprise*, upon which her owner, Mike Vanderbilt, had spared no expense.

Designed by Starling Burgess, *Enterprise* was 80 ft on the waterline and carried rather more sail than Shamrock's 7,500 sq ft; she had an unusual circular alloy mast made of duralumin – very expensive but light – while *Shamrock* bore the weight of a hollowed-spruce mast of elliptical section, a difference that might well have worked against *Shamrock* from the start. *Enterprise* was well mechanized throughout, having an unusually constructed main boom by which the sail's curvature could to some extent be controlled – a feature that was to prove most useful. Vanderbilt himself took the helm of *Enterprise* for this, the fourteenth challenge, with Sherman Hoyt in reserve. Also in the crew was 'Bubbles' Havemayer, with Captain Workman aboard as representative of the Royal Ulster Yacht Club, whose challenge, on behalf of Lipton, this was. Aboard *Shamrock* Captain Ned Heard took the helm, last of the professional yachtmasters to do so in a race for the America's Cup. The designer, Charles Nicholson, and his son were also aboard, with Captain Duncan Neill as owner's representative, while navigation was in the hands of Captain Paul. Representing the New York Yacht Club was Johnson de Forest, a man of much knowledge in regard to the rules of racing.

RIGHT The building of
Sopwith's *Endeavour* in
Camper and Nicholson's yard.

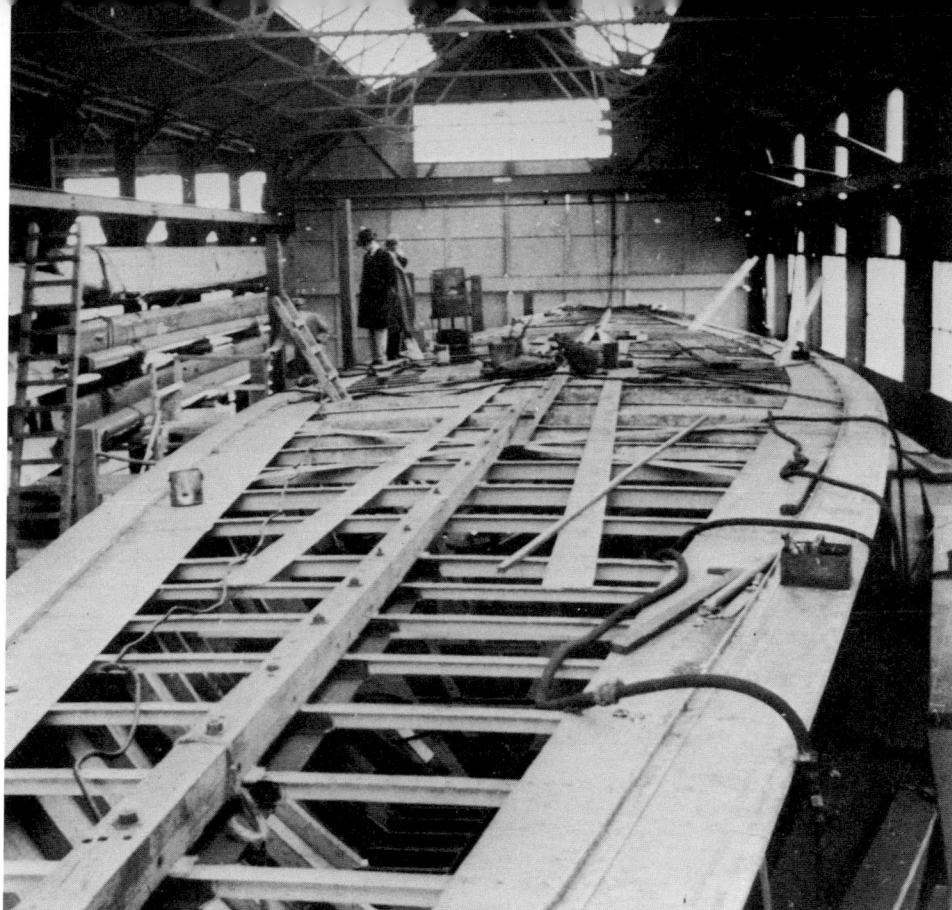

BELOW Working sail aboard
Endeavour; many deckhands
were employed in the great
racers of the 1930s. Sopwith,
an experienced helmsman, can
be seen at the wheel.

The fourteenth challenge was to start on a new course, off Rhode Island, where all such races have been held since, the old Long Island Sound course having become too full of shipping for good sailing or safety. The weather was fine, and for some while the racers stayed level, but it was not long before *Enterprise* pulled ahead after luffing out, and came round the mark well in front of *Shamrock*, sailing at her and causing her to bear away and lose time. *Enterprise* won the first of the series by a clear three minutes.

In the second race, *Enterprise* was again the winner, this time by some six minutes; she also won the third when Shamrock parted a main halyard. The fourth race, run with a fresher wind than before, once again went to the defender.

Before the next challenge was issued Sir Thomas Lipton had died, and a great racing character was removed from the yachting scene. Characters spring eternal, however, and by 1934 T. O. M. Sopwith was in with a challenge, coming on to the big-yacht stage just when the sheer expense of racing such boats seemed set fair to prevent any further challenges.

Sopwith, already known in amateur racing circles, was a much experienced helmsman with a first-class showing in the 12-metre boats – *Mouette* being one of his best-known yachts at that time. *Endeavour*, with which he challenged, was 83 ft on the waterline, 130 ft overall, with a 21-ft beam, a draught of 14½ ft and something over 7,500 sq ft of sail. She was built by Camper and Nicholson. Her rival in the fifteenth challenge was to be *Rainbow*, owned by a syndicate that included Harold Vanderbilt. Designed by Starling Burgess, *Rainbow* carried as much sail as *Endeavour* but used the new duralumin mast, as did *Enterprise*; she was fitted with many innovations that put her ahead of *Endeavour*, the American designers being as ever a jump ahead of the British. *Rainbow* had only just conformed to the rules in regard to her below-deck fittings, and there was some argument that led to both defender and challenger removing some of their contrivances. On 15 September the first race in the series started off Newport, Rhode Island, with Lady Sopwith aboard *Endeavour* as observer, together with Charles Nicholson the designer, Frank Murdoch, skipper Williams, Captain Paul navigating, and, thanks to a last-minute strike in England by the paid hands, a wholly amateur crew. *Rainbow* was carrying a professional Scandinavian crew. The first race was found to be up against the time limit and was abandoned with *Rainbow* in the lead. It was held again two days later in a fair wind, which suited Sopwith well enough though the swell was troublesome; because of this he was given a delay of 15 minutes for his mainsail to be hoisted. At the start *Rainbow* went ahead, with *Endeavour* a mere 18 seconds behind at the mark; and *Endeavour* came home two minutes ahead.

In the second of the series there was again a fair wind and *Endeavour*, on the lee side, took the lead and maintained it fractionally for some eight miles, but on the windward stretch *Rainbow* went ahead, *Endeavour* overstood a little and, though suffering the loss of a genoa, came home just over 50 seconds in the lead, establishing at the same time a record for the distance.

Miraculous! British hopes rose high: two wins in a row, the Cup theirs

ABOVE LEFT *Jolie Brise*, a pilot boat from Le Havre, in the Fastnet race of 1928. ABOVE RIGHT Mike Vanderbilt's cutter *Enterprise*, defender in the America's Cup series of 1930 against Lipton's J-class *Shamrock V*. LEFT *Ranger*, Vanderbilt-owned, a super-J-class vessel designed by Starling Burgess and Olin Stephens. Her spinnaker covered two-fifths of an acre. BELOW *Vim*, a Vanderbilt boat in the 12-metre class which was replacing the stately J-class by 1939.

so far. But elation came too soon: in the third race *Endeavour* went well ahead from the starting line and passed the first mark with six minutes in hand, *Rainbow* having had trouble with her spinnaker. Aboard *Rainbow* Sherman Hoyt was at the helm and at the first mark he luffed, coming almost close-hauled; Sopwith tacked across in *Rainbow*'s direction in an attempt to come right ahead, but muffed the manœuvre and allowed *Rainbow* to head directly for the finish and win by nearly three-and-a-half minutes. In the fourth race some tricky manœuvring at the start got *Rainbow* away nicely but she was caught up with by *Endeavour* at the first mark. Even so, *Endeavour* was overtaken soon after, *Rainbow* being on the weather side. Sopwith luffed up but the American gave no way and forced *Endeavour* to take avoiding action; on crossing the finish line, *Endeavour* was wearing the protest flag as she came in one minute behind *Rainbow*. Under English procedure it is enough to hoist the protest flag at the finish, but Sopwith's protest was refused a hearing by the Race Committee who were of the opinion that the flag should have been hoisted at the time of the occurrence. This is a controversy that has never been settled to this day, and although the Race Committee were strictly correct on a technicality, even some American opinion expressed misgivings. Sopwith himself was outspoken about it.

Each of the yachts now had two wins to its credit; after the fourth race *Rainbow* added to her ballast and this appeared to improve her handling. On 29 September the fifth in the series took place in a moderate wind. *Rainbow* went ahead from the start and continued to increase her lead. Although she lost a man overboard – and recovered him – she finished four minutes ahead.

Protest flags were flying from both yachts at the start of the final race, but these were later withdrawn. *Endeavour* pulled away well at the start, but *Rainbow* caught up on the first leg and was leading at the first mark. *Endeavour* was carrying too much headsail at this point and *Rainbow* went smartly through while Sopwith shifted to working sails. After coming round the weather mark for the finishing line, *Endeavour*, after some initial trouble with her spinnaker, began to overhaul and reduced the lead sharply. Aboard *Rainbow* the helm was now handed over to Sherman Hoyt who bore away to leeward. This proved a snare for Sopwith, who made an attempt to take the American's wind. Hoyt was ahead by no more than a whisker when he luffed and took a safe position to leeward and came home the winner by 55 seconds.

So the great *Endeavour* had failed, and she did not try again: she was ultimately presented to the Maritime Trust Museum by Sir Thomas Sopwith.

Endeavour II entered Sopwith's service in 1936; at 228 tons she was his largest boat yet, built to the class-permitted maximum. Her overall length was no less than 135 ft (87 ft on the waterline) with a 21½-ft beam, a 15-ft draught, and a sail area in excess of 7,500 sq ft. In her first season she performed reasonably well and took a number of prizes, but lost her mast during a race at the Plymouth regatta, possibly because she was injudiciously raced in blustery weather with unreefed sails. (In fact it was not uncommon

RIGHT The racing yacht
Britannia.

BELOW *Britannia* on the
stocks. Under royal
ownership, latterly of George
v, she held the world record
for the number of races won.

for the J-boats to lose their masts, the reason being a rule defect in so far as the masts and rigging were of less seaworthy standards than the hulls. The yachts were capable of such high speeds through the water that there was a drag, or stress, laid upon the masts.) *Endeavour II* challenged the American *Ranger*, known as a super-J, for the sixteenth challenge in 1937. *Ranger*, another Vanderbilt boat, was a brilliant yacht designed by Starling Burgess in co-operation with a newcomer, Olin Stephens, a young man who was to make a deep mark on yacht design. *Ranger* held the distinction of having the world's largest sail area: a spinnaker of an incredible two-fifths of an acre – 18,000 sq ft.

The sixteenth challenge was to be the last of the America's Cup series in which the J-class featured, for their reign was in fact not long. The first race of the series took place at the end of July 1937; aboard *Endeavour II* were Sopwith at the helm, Lady Sopwith again observing, Squadron-Leader Jim Scarlett as navigator, with Charles Nicholson, Frank J. Murdoch, Tom Thorneycroft and the skipper George Williams. In that first race *Ranger* sped ahead from the start in light conditions and thrashed *Endeavour* by an amazing 17 minutes. In the second race *Ranger* excelled herself: this time her lead was 18½ minutes. On the third race matters went a little better for Britain: *Ranger*'s lead was cut to four minutes, possibly because Sopwith had removed some ballast, put his yacht on the slips and had her re-polished. But the fourth race again went to *Ranger* when *Endeavour* was recalled after crossing the start line too early.

Thus ended until after the Second World War Britain's hopes of regaining the America's Cup. The war finished off the whole of the J-class: by the time it was over, their sheer size had become too expensive to crew and there were too few rich men left. It is a matter for regret that those great yachts have gone, like the great clippers and windjammers of an earlier age, with their towering canvas and richly appointed accommodation. They were impressive in their graceful beauty and their very size, and nothing like them will ever be seen again.

Sopwith and Vanderbilt did in fact race one another again: in 1939 they had a last fling before the outbreak of war. Sopwith's 12-metre *Tomahawk* raced Vanderbilt's *Vim* which was shipped across the Atlantic to compete; *Vim* finished the season as the best in the 12-metre class.

Perhaps one of the most famous names in yachting history is that of the cutter *Britannia*. Owned originally by King Edward VII, she was a sister-ship of Lord Dunraven's *Valkyrie* and of the United States cutter *Navahoe*. Designed in 1893 by G. L. Watson and built on the Clyde, she had a most notable career, lasting until 1935 when she was finally laid to rest. Originally cutter-rigged, she was re-rigged five times in all; she was of 115.02 tons net register (221 tons gross), 112 ft overall length, 89-ft 5-in waterline, with a 23-ft 7-in beam and a 16-ft 3-in draught; her mast was 164 ft from truck to deck. Of light construction, she was tasteful and comfortable throughout: her fittings were of polished yellow pine and mahogany, while rich tapestries and cretonnes decked her four guest cabins. On the starboard side just aft of amidships was a large saloon and the owner's cabin with a swinging cot. Just forward was the messroom for the racing crew of 30 hands, with stairs to the upper deck, also two lavatories – one for guests and one for crew – and a washbasin for the use of the owner and his guests, plus the owner's own bathroom and lavatory. There were bunks for the crew along the sides, together with lockers, cabinets, dressers, a store-room and pantry, and a separate cabin for the skipper.

Britannia was often sailed by George V, the King acting as helmsman, and skippered by that well-known character Major Sir Philip Hunloke, who was the King's Representative aboard and King's sailing master. Hunloke was a brilliant and often daring helmsman who disliked the professionals, considering that they played too much for a win rather than for good sportsmanship; though he got along well with one of them, skipper Albert Barr Turner; in their first season together the King's yacht won 23 flags in 26 races, 11 of them firsts. *Britannia* was the world's most raced and most successful yacht, winning her hundredth race on 6 August 1930 when sailed by Sir Philip Hunloke with the King embarked. After the death of George V in 1936, the old yacht was taken out into the English Channel under tow of two destroyers and sunk by the detonation of charges placed in her bilges.

The regatta week held annually in August at Cowes was – and to a muted extent still is – a glittering sea occasion. Royalty, more especially in the days of Victoria, Edward VII and George V, made a point of attending aboard the royal yacht *Victoria and Albert*. A battleship was provided as guardship by the Royal Navy, with attendant destroyers and minesweepers, in those more spacious times (today a frigate performs the duty). There were permanent buoys provided for the mooring of the *Victoria and Albert* and the racing yacht *Britannia*, and Cowes harbour was crammed with bobbing masts and spars; at least until 1939 the terraces and clubrooms of the Royal Yacht Squadron at the edge of the harbour were filled with immaculately dressed yachtsmen and their ladies, most of them from the aristocracy and gentry, all of them wealthy. Titled society brought its pleasure yachts to Osborne Bay, the Medina, Gurnard's Bay ... every foreign flag would be there, and the Parade crowded with spectators and holidaymakers, watching at night the tremendous firework displays which began when the King fired a salvo of rockets from the royal yacht. In the 1890s the Eleven Royal Brighton Minstrels came with the Pierrot Troupe to give shows. Girls strolled along sporting yacht ribbons in red, white and blue on their hats; even dogs had their day of fashion at Cowes: one year it would be collies, another scotties, schipperkes, French poodles or the plain English fox-terrier. Famous names were present: Lipton, Sopwith, Pierpont Morgan, the Vanderbilts, the Astors, and Lily Langtry in the days of her reign as the King's mistress and friend. Rank and money abounded: foreign royalties – the Kaiser and the Tsar among them – proliferated. Cowes maintained a delightful garden-party atmosphere for the Week, with none of the pomp and brass bands so characteristic of Germany's Kiel Regatta.

Cowes Week provided and still provides the stage for the Admiral's Cup races. These consist of the Channel Race of 220 miles, the Fastnet of 605 miles and two 30-mile races round the Solent.

RIGHT George V and his party on *Britannia*'s deck during Cowes Week, 1928.

BELOW Cowes Week, August 1900, a grand social occasion. At the end of the lawn is the R.Y.S. landing-stage; the royal yacht *Victoria and Albert* can be seen in the distance.

In recent times the social shine has rather come off Cowes Week and there is perhaps less emphasis on that aspect than on the sheer hard work necessary to provision and overhaul boats for the Fastnet, jobs which in easier times would have been largely left to the paid hands. But in yachting hard work is part of the enjoyment, and nothing can wholly dim the splendour of the occasion.

5 Post-War Racing and the America's Cup

The big international classes that used to be seen at Cowes Regatta and other notable events had all gone after the Second World War – the Js, and nearly all the 12s and 8s as well. The huge cruising yachts had also vanished, leaving a trail of glory – and bills that could no longer be met. On the other side of the picture, as the pressures of life ashore began to drive more and more people to seek peace on the sea, cruising as well as racing received a boost, though by this time cruising was done mainly in small motor yachts.

Modern materials – nylon and other synthetics instead of rope and canvas – have eased the sailor's burden (terylene and dacron, for instance, make excellent sails), and plastic fittings have taken a lot of labour out of domestic matters.

Designers such as Uffa Fox, John Illingworth and Stephens in the United States, were the fathers of today's ocean racer: they designed safe, seaworthy craft that the more-or-less ordinary citizen could afford to buy and sail. Gone was the need for large professional crews of 30 or more – who, in any case, were no longer there for the hiring.

So, small was left: the 6-metre yachts, declared obsolescent by the International Yacht Racing Union, were very thin on the water at Cowes by 1953 – only a handful took part in the events, though there was still an interest in the class in America. Coming along in the fifties was the 5·5-metre class which was cheaper to run. The Dragon class, designed by Knud Reimers, had also made its debut, the Duke of Edinburgh's wedding-present *Bluebottle* being an early example. The National Swallow class too had advanced in 1947, and later came the X's, the Victory class, the Flying Fifteens, the Bembridge Redwings, the West Solent One-Design and the Q-class.

Since yacht rig and design has always tended to reflect the age in which the vessel is built, dinghy classes were becoming more and more popular: the 14-ft International class that race in the Itchenor Gallon and the Prince of Wales' Cup, the National 12-ft class, the Fireflies, Fireballs, Mirrors, Scorpions, National Merlin Rocket, International Sharpie and the National Swordfish. In 1953 the Round the Island Race sponsored by the Royal Corinthian Yacht Club was instituted for dinghy classes, the 'Island' being of course the Isle of Wight. (Back in 1926 the Round the Island Race for larger vessels had been instituted, and now attracts very large numbers of entries.) The course is 64 miles; and the first dinghy race attracted 196 starters in the six classes. A cup is presented for the first home and other trophies are competed for. The Olympic classes are specially designed for use in the Olympic Games, of which yacht racing has been a part since 1900, when Paris was the venue and the racing took place on the Seine. These classes include Tempeste, designed by Ian Proctor of Britain; Tornado, designed by another Briton, Rodney March; Flying Dutchman, designed by Uffa van Essen of the Netherlands; Soling, by Jan Linge of Norway, and Finn, by Richard Sarly of Finland.

In 1972, with typical German efficiency and painstaking enthusiasm, a magnificent harbour was especially constructed for the Olympic Games on Kiel Fiord, a most elaborate affair with special flats to accommodate the yacht crews and every facility provided for the press, plus a plethora of official passes. The harbour and its amenities are still in use for regattas and day-to-day yachting.

After the war thoughts turned once again to the America's Cup and the possibilities of at last bringing it back to Britain. Preliminary discussions took place in 1946 between Captain John Illingworth, Commodore of the Royal Ocean Racing Club, and de Courcy Fales, the New York Yacht Club commodore. The day of the great J-class being over, the possibilities of small craft with an approximate 48-ft waterline length were considered. But it was not until 1956 that the discussions between Sir Ralph Gore, commodore of the Royal Yacht Squadron, and Mr Henry Sears, by then commodore of the NYYC, gave birth to a new concept of racers for the Cup. Among other rule changes the waterline length was reduced and the old rule that the challenging vessel must herself sail across to America was cut out. This led to the 12-metre class becoming the choice for the new challenge.

In June 1957 the Royal Yacht Squadron issued its first post-war challenge for the Cup. Out of the eight submitted designs from four British designers, David Boyd's was chosen: *Sceptre*, built at Sandbank in Argyll by Robertson's, was a yacht of advanced design, a brand-new feature being the large, open cockpit – both for sheltering the crew and giving navigator and helmsman a much-improved view across clear decks. *Sceptre* was launched in April 1958 and was raced against Owen Aisher's *Evaine*, brought out and refitted to act as trial boat. Even though *Evaine* was not one of the best of her 12-metre class, *Sceptre* never managed to outsail her convincingly; as a result there was much depression in British racing circles, although later in the season she put up better performances when her sails were replaced with heavier material than the terylene cloth which had originally been fitted.

In the meantime the defenders across the Atlantic were busy making their choice between four alternatives, all fine yachts: *Columbia*, designed by Olin Stephens of Sparkman and Stephens, New York, launched in June 1958 from the Nevins Yard for the Henry Sears syndicate; *Weatherly*,

LEFT Uffa Fox, designer, yachtsman, friend and one-time sailing mentor to Prince Philip.

RIGHT Prince Philip at the helm of his Dragon-class yacht *Bluebottle* in the Solent. Lieutenant-Commander Michael Crichton is with him in the cockpit.

BELOW Cowes Week, 1966: contestants at the start of the Round the Island race.

designed by Phil Rhodes, and launched in the same month; *Easterner*, designed by C. Raymond Hunt and owned by Chandler Hovey; and the pre-war *Vim*, now refitted and brought back into service. This wide choice of first-class vessels really gave the defenders the advantage from the start, since *Sceptre* had never been in such intense competition and thus had not been brought to so fine a pitch of readiness.

Lengthy observation trials were held between the four contenders for the honour, and after the final series in September 1958 the choice was settled: *Columbia* was to defend, although the old *Vim* was a very close second.

While the American observation trials were in progress, *Sceptre* arrived at Newport for working up, something that was far from successfully carried out. All she had to sharpen her teeth against was an aged yacht, the *Gleam*, which had an auxiliary engine whose screw acted as a drag on her speed and forced *Sceptre* to trail buckets astern to keep her own speed down.

On the morning of the first race, the sky was overcast and there was a light wind from the north; the race was to be run over the windward-leeward course and, with Commander Joe Brooks navigating, Commander Graham Mann at the helm and a professional, Stanley Bishop, in charge of the hands, *Sceptre* had no difficulty at the start. However *Columbia*, with Briggs Cunningham at the helm, was more than seven minutes in the lead by the first mark, though *Sceptre* closed the gap on rounding the Cup buoy. But there was no luck: *Columbia* romped home by seven-and-a-half minutes.

The next race was over the triangular course and again *Sceptre* started well, crossing the line to leeward, but soon *Columbia* had pulled ahead. Then for a period both yachts were becalmed; when the wind came back *Sceptre* hoisted her Herbulot spinnaker and took the lead, passing the first mark with nearly two minutes in hand. But on a freshening wind *Columbia* drew abeam and flew on to win – in fact, with *Columbia* ahead, the race was abandoned when the fickle wind once again failed, but an American win was recorded. In the third race the American crossed the finishing line almost eleven-and-a-half minutes ahead, and the challengers lost heart. In the fourth *Columbia* led by a little over eight minutes. In the next Graham Mann jumped the starting gun but returned brilliantly, though he was forced to leave *Columbia* to windward. Soon after, *Sceptre* jammed a genoa cleat which affected the handling of the spinnaker and *Columbia* took the first mark with five-and-a-half minutes in hand; then *Sceptre* parted her spinnaker guy and for a while suffered a wind-spilled sail. After this, it not being *Sceptre*'s day, her aluminium boom broke. This was disaster, but *Sceptre*'s crew fought on and caught up a little, but not enough to win the final leg. So once again the America's Cup remained in the New York Yacht Club's keeping.

In 1960 the Royal Sydney Yacht Squadron issued a challenge, the first ever to come from Australia, the race to take place in 1962. Australian yachtsmen had little experience of the 12-metre class but as citizens of a young and vigorous country much given to sailing – Sydney harbour always seems to be teeming with yachts, often to the concern of the masters of the great liners – they were expected to put up a first-class performance. Although Britain's nose had been put out of joint (the Royal Thames Yacht Club had hoped to challenge themselves), it cannot be denied that the infusion of new blood was expected to bring back interest in a race that had become a disheartening succession of American wins.

Gretel, built by Lars Halvorsen at Ryde in New South Wales and launched in 1962, was to be the challenger. In the meantime the New York Yacht Club had published a memorandum setting forth its views on the forthcoming race, and indicating that if they (the NYYC) should win, then a challenge from the Royal Thames, or a substitute British club if requested, would be accepted for 1963 or the following year. If the Sydney club should win, then the NYYC would stand aside and permit a British club to challenge the Royal Sydney Yacht Squadron. This was a generous gesture that ensured Britain's chance to re-enter the races for the Cup.

In March the work-up began in Sydney with *Vim* as trial boat, and after a number of the usual teething troubles *Gretel* began to show as a fine racer. Her bow was much finer than *Sceptre*'s and she had a wide, flat counter which would give her greater waterline length in a seaway.

In America the competition for the defence began in earnest during August, the contenders being the new 12-metre *Nefertiti*, Boston-built for the Ross Anderson syndicate, *Columbia*, the 1958 defender, and once again *Weatherly* and *Easterner*. As ever, the Americans were leaving nothing to chance and were putting in all they had got with their usual efficiency and forethought. The final choice was *Weatherly*, under the helmsmanship of Bus Mosbacher.

Amid interest that had grown steadily since the challenge was issued, and with more spectators than ever before, the first Australian challenge was met on 15 September, President Kennedy watching from a destroyer of the United States Navy. Aircraft flew overhead and a dirigible of the US Coastguard hovered like an airborne sausage. After the first race, which *Weatherly* won by three minutes 46 seconds, it seemed as though the old, old story was to be repeated and, as ever, despondency settled in a cloud over the challengers. But this early despondency was not altogether justified: in the next race, over the triangular course on 16 September, in a very fresh breeze, *Gretel*, after *Weatherly* had gone through her lee near the start and achieved a five-length lead, inched up on the defender, which rounded the mark with just 14 seconds in hand – and then broke her spinnaker boom. *Gretel*, hoisting her own spinnaker, went past with a flourish. *Weatherly* by now had lost just too much time, and the Australians came home 47 seconds ahead to win the first race since 1934 when Sopwith had achieved a victory over *Rainbow*. Naturally enough, the Australian supporters went mad and everything afloat in the vicinity sounded its siren. But the next race two days later went to the defenders, *Gretel* being late on a tack and allowing *Weatherly* into the leeward position: *Weatherly*'s time was eight minutes, 40 seconds shorter.

On 22 September *Weatherly* just made it: the fourth race was held in very light air, again over the triangular course, and *Weatherly* took the lead from the start. *Gretel* caught up between the first and second marks;

ABOVE *Sceptre*, challenger for the America's Cup in 1958. RIGHT *Weatherly*, skippered by Arthur Knapp, was America's Cup defender in 1962, when Australia issued the challenge. She is seen close-hauled on the starboard tack. BELOW The 1958 America's Cup: *Sceptre* (left) and *Columbia*, the defender.

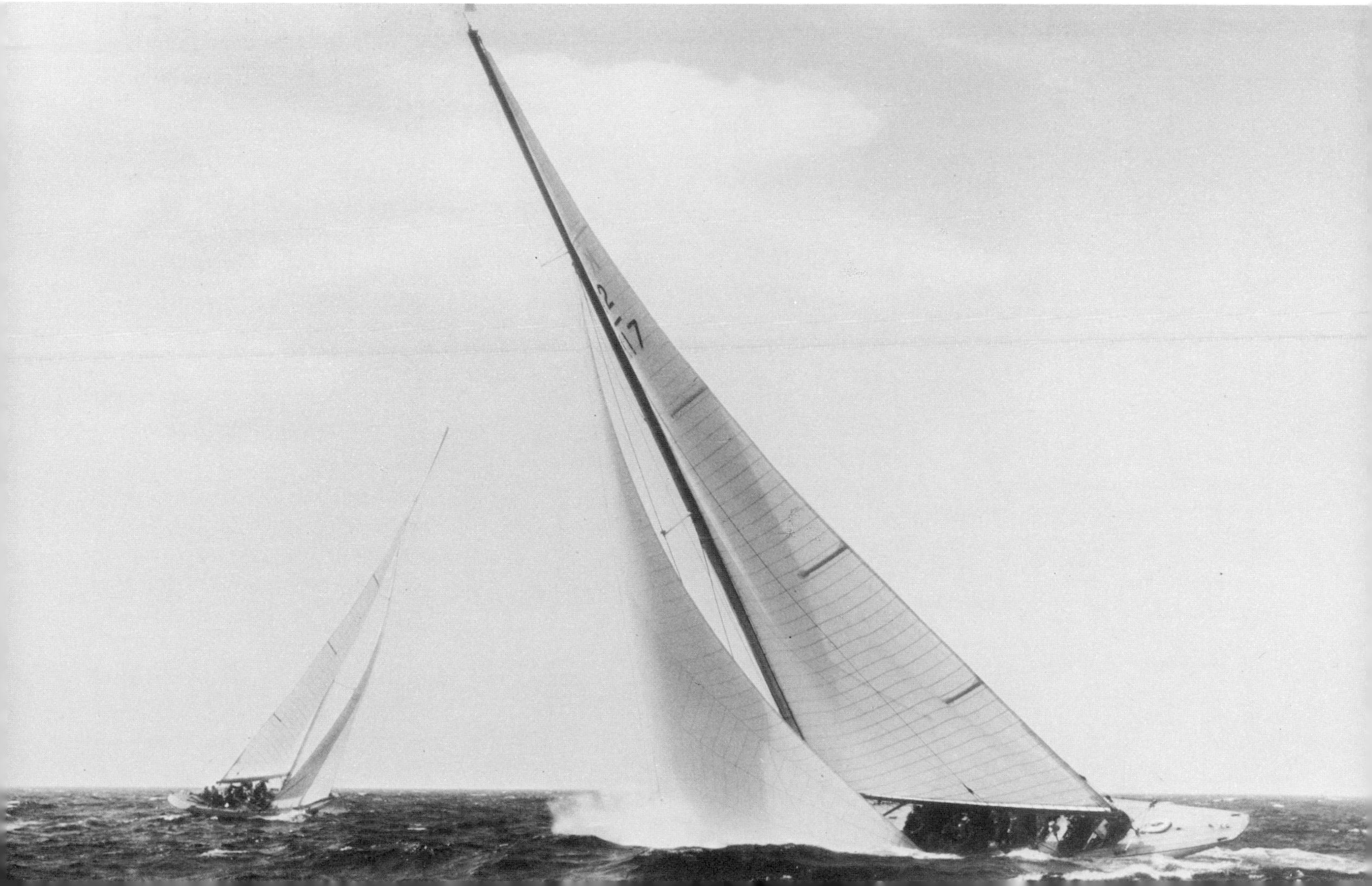

with only a length or so between them both yachts swept on for the line, but with *Weatherly* holding to windward and shaking out her spinnaker, she won by 26 seconds. And the fifth and last race was also won by the defenders, with a lead of a little more than three-and-a-half minutes. Once again the Cup remained firmly in American hands. Nevertheless, the Australians had put up a real challenge, their crewing had been superb, and there was every reason for them to feel satisfaction in having brought new interest to the sport.

In 1964 Britain came back, challenging with *Sovereign* against *Constellation*'s defence; this series ended badly for Britain, with some fairly wretched times being put up. The next challenge came in 1967, once more from Australia, when their *Dame Pattie* raced *Intrepid* with what had become over the years the inevitable result: another win for America, where the Cup had remained ever since that first race when Queen Victoria, aboard the royal yacht at Cowes, had received the report from her signalman: '*America* first, Your Majesty. There is no second.' The future was to bring more challenges: Australia again, the Royal Dorset Yacht Club, Baron Bisch's French syndicate; but no-one seemed able to wrest the Cup from the New York Yacht Club.

Edward Heath's first ocean race was the Cowes to Dinard in *Clarion of Wight* owned by Maurice Laing, a yacht that had already won the Fastnet. His own *Morning Cloud*, designed by Sparkman and Stephens of New York and launched in the Medway in April 1969, was to become one of the great sailers in the 700-mile Sydney–Hobart race, in which she made her debut at the very end of her launching year. This was the twenty-fifth occasion of the great Australian race across the stormy Bass Strait to Tasmania; in the first race, out of only nine starters, eight had disappeared into a raging gale and were feared lost.

Morning Cloud was 34 ft overall and built of glass fibre, teak-finished below. She was well fitted out inside with six bunks convertible into seats; amidships was a chart-table, galley and dining table. Mr Heath brought her into the Derwent River for Hobart five days out from Sydney Heads to become the only British winner since Captain Illingworth, in his 34-ft 9-in cutter *Rani* (designed by A. L. Barber of Sydney), had won the first race in 1945.

The Sydney–Hobart is but one event in a series of races for the Southern Cross Cup. December, Australia's midsummer month, was the chosen time. On this occasion in 1969 the Royal Ocean Racing Club was represented by *Crusade* owned by Sir Max Aitken, *Prospect of Whitby* owned by Arthur Slater, and *Morning After*, sister yacht of *Morning Cloud*, owned by Rodney Hill. *Morning Cloud* was to be the reserve; her crew included Owen Parker, already well acquainted with the boat, as sailing master, Anthony Churchill, navigator, and Jean Berger at the helm, plus another helmsman, Sammy Sampson, a tough farmer and experienced yachtsman.

The race was started at 1100 hours on 26 December by the Australian Prime Minister from aboard a frigate of the Royal Australian Navy, with 79 yachts competing – a record. The whole of Sydney Harbour from the

OPPOSITE Hundreds of yards of fine cloth go into the making of a spinnaker; the strains to which it is subjected and its potential for 'blowing out' make it a valuable friend of the sailmaker.

OVERLEAF *Morning Cloud*, with Edward Heath at the helm, in the Solent during Cowes Week, 1977.

Heads inwards seethed with spectator boats, some thousands of them, all set to sail or motor amongst the competitors as soon as they got under way; nevertheless the start itself was kept well cleared of intrusive craft and the competitors got away, with Edward Heath at the helm of *Morning Cloud*. He made the Heads after some tacking as he closed, and, spectator boats or not, sped for the open sea under the eyes of massed land-bound spectators on the Heads and slopes.

Morning Cloud came out into a strong wind from the north-north-east and, with the spinnaker set, cleared away into the ocean swell usually to be encountered outside the Heads. There was around 20 knots of wind now and the sun was shining, a splendid day for the start. It was decided to try to find the warm southerly current flowing farther out to sea: this was a two-knot set that would help carry them on faster, and *Morning Cloud* picked up the current some 60 miles out. Incoming radio reports indicated *Crusade* and *Apollo* (the latter a 57-ft yacht owned by Alan Bond of Perth and designed by Bob Miller) much closer in to the New South Wales coast – in fact the shorter course – while another indicated *Morning After* as being to seaward of *Morning Cloud*; but soon after this *Morning After* was reported as moving coastwards again.

Morning Cloud sped south, making ten knots and more at times, gybing now and again and maintaining her distance off shore; but on the fourth day out from the Heads the wind dropped and the spinnaker came down to be replaced by the floater spinnaker, though soon there was not sufficient wind to fill it. *Morning Cloud* lay in the doldrums until a light and very variable breeze came up faintly. However, the radio had been indicating a likely blow from southerly, though the reports from Tasmania ahead were confusing, some suggesting a south-easterly wind and others a south-westerly. For *Morning Cloud*'s purposes, the former would be vastly better in her well off-shore position; with it she could tack in for Tasmania.

While a strong wind had been forecast, what *Morning Cloud* got was a full gale shrieking up from the Antarctic ice, bringing with it more than a taste of those terrible ever-frozen regions at the bottom of the world. Fortunately, the gale was south-easterly; headsails were shifted and the main reefed as the wind came up to some 40 knots with gusts beyond that. A very heavy sea was running. The crews were soaked through in no time and might well have imagined themselves aboard a windjammer trying to make the stormy passage of the Horn. Visibility came down and so did the rain – indeed hailstones flailed the crew as they fought *Morning Cloud* into the wind's teeth. There followed the darkness and the intensely bitter cold of the High South latitudes. There was no hot food or drink for the crew – and the bilges began to fill; the heavy inflow of water was too much for the pumps, and hand-baling had to begin.

Some relief came to the weary, cold men with the dawn when more sail was sent aloft; the outline of the Tasmanian coast began to come up and with it the landfall of the Organ Pipes, a weirdly shaped high promontory. Here a tricky wind, which has a curious siphoning effect, flows across the top to trap unwary seamen. Luckily the wind then backed to the south and *Morning Cloud* sailed into Storm Bay and to the line, 51 minutes

OPPOSITE The Admiral's Cup series of 1969: *Prospect of Whitby* in the foreground competing in the Cowes to Dinard race.

ABOVE The crew of the British vessel *Sovereign*; she challenged for the 1964 America's Cup but lost to *Constellation*.

RIGHT The start of the 1969 Sydney to Hobart race.

and a few seconds ahead of *Prospect of Whitby*, thus winning the race for Britain.

The prestigious Britannia Cup, presented in 1950 by George VI for ocean racers, re-stimulated interest in the great occasion of Cowes Week which after the war had begun to degenerate into a round-the-buoys affair. And in 1957 the first of the Admiral's Cup series was held; a £300-cup was given by Sir Myles Wyatt, then the owner of *Bloodhound* which later passed to the Duke of Edinburgh. The series was opened by the Channel Race – 225 miles from Southsea, east of the Royal Sovereign Light, across to Le Havre and back – which counted double points. Single points (until 1971) were awarded in the two inshore races – the Britannia Cup and the New York Yacht Club Cup – and triple points in the Fastnet.

Edward Heath took the second of his *Morning Cloud*s into the Admiral's Cup in 1971 after more Australian racing the year before. *Morning Cloud II*'s birth was due in part to Mr Heath's need of a bigger boat so as to qualify for entry in the Admiral's Cup; he had followed the advice of that experienced yachtsman and designer Uffa Fox (until his death in 1972 a man inextricably part of Cowes and Cowes Week and a personal friend of the Duke of Edinburgh and the Prince of Wales) to build a boat of more than 40 ft overall. For this he went to the Cowes boatyard of Clare Lallow with a design by Olin Stephens of Sparkman and Stephens. The new boat took the water in April 1971 and very beautiful she was. The teething troubles were few and in she went for the June trials for the Admiral's Cup; she was chosen for the team, which included *Cervantes II* and *Prospect of Whitby*, with *Quailo* in reserve. Edward Heath captained the team and was thus landed with the job (in addition to those of race-winning and Premiership) of collecting all the various necessities and of arranging the administrative work.

In the first place, a team leader must crew his own yacht with the right people, and this raises many problems: first, there must be inter-reliability and compatibility, each member having a strong competitive spirit. Anything less can be disastrous. There must be guts and toughness and the ability to disregard the often disturbing noise of waves and wind; there must be the skills of seamanship, navigation and helm-handling; the navigator must be fully familiar with his various aids such as charts and tides, and the skipper must be prepared to go without sleep since, like the master of any ocean-going vessel, he is in effect always on watch. There must be full knowledge among the crew of the equipment and its use, of the functions and limitations of the sails and their gear, and generally of electronics; and there must be an ability to effect running repairs. Only a small number of people are available who have all this competence and know-how; and some of them may not have a husband or wife willing to allow them week-end after week-end, or find it possible to take time off from work in this workaday age. Then there is the provisioning, the planning overall, the organization of watches at sea and the general running of the boat. Mr Heath had plenty to do. Fortunately he is a man of ideas, accustomed to solving sudden problems, a man who has that valuable quality, possessed by most deep-sea professional seamen, an ability to improvise.

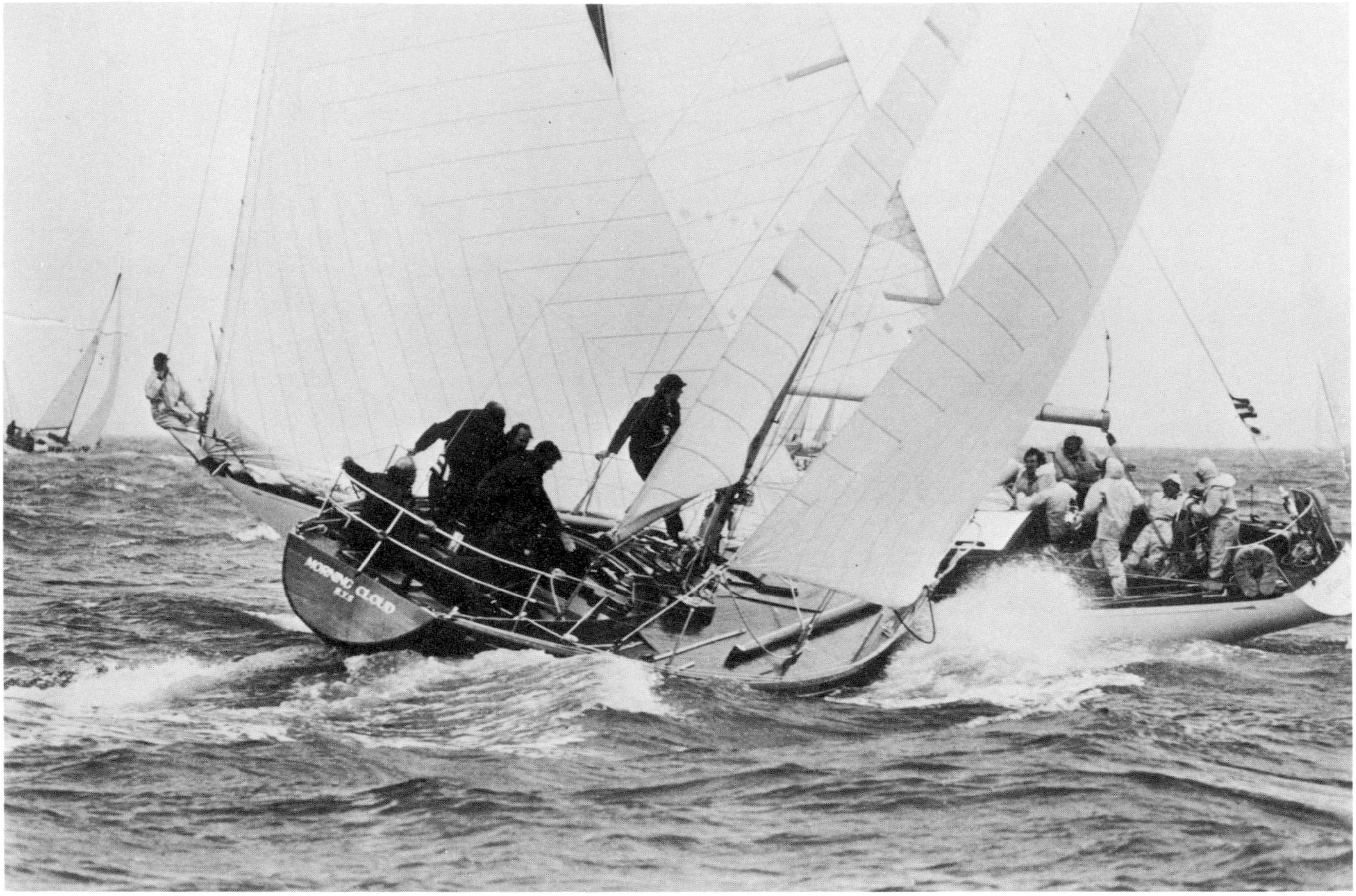
MORNING CLOUD

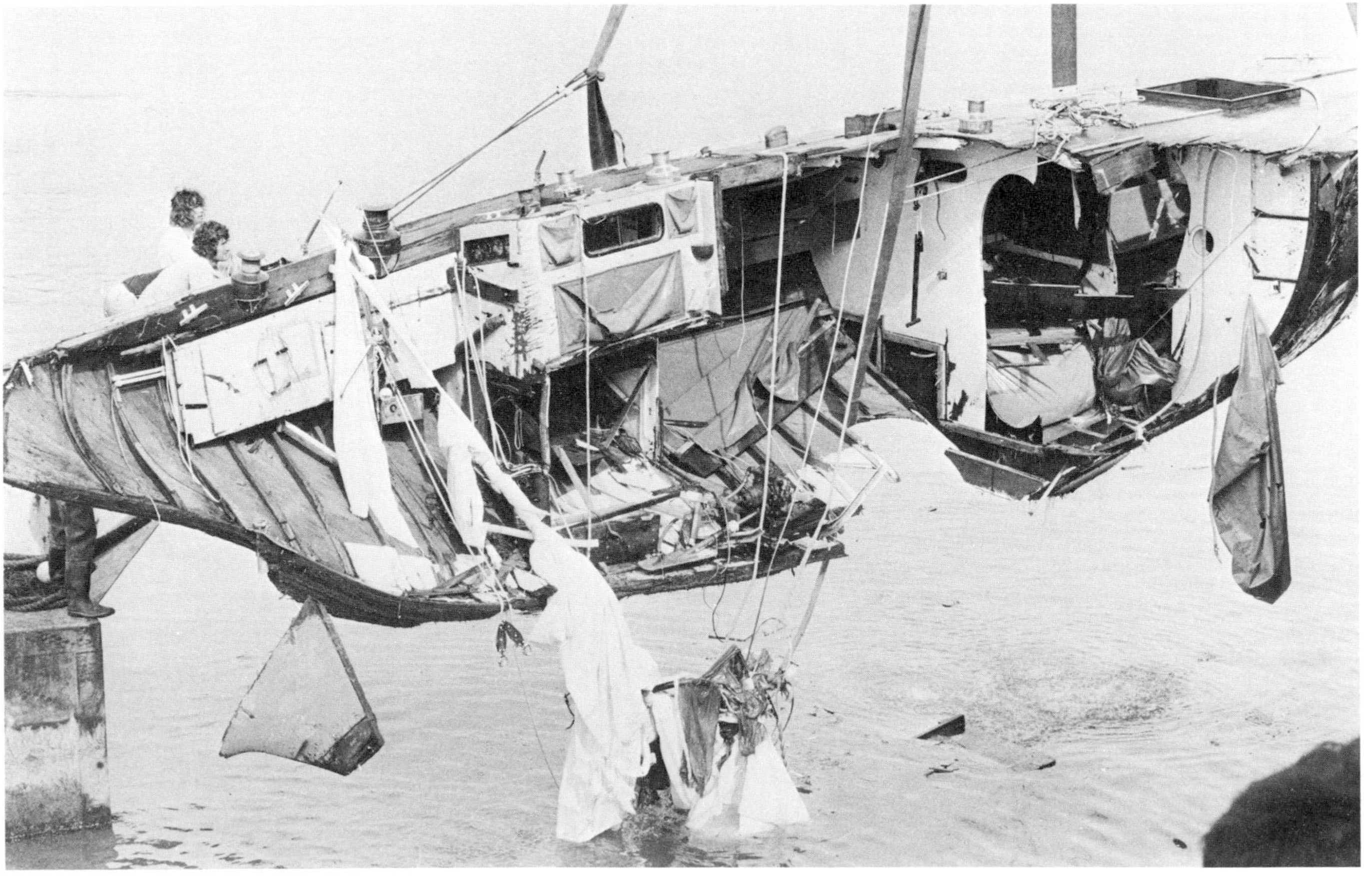

The series began with the Channel Race, and *Morning Cloud II* was placed third with *Prospect of Whitby* first. Heath's team won 270 points, thus leading from both Australia and America. As the lapel buttons had it, Ted was Ahead. However, the British lead over America was soon cut from 36 points to a mere nine, and her lead over Australia cut to 37 points from 54, partly owing to the disqualification of *Cervantes II* and partly to *Morning Cloud* finishing fourth in the first of the short races while Mr Heath was attending the House of Commons for an important debate. Two days later, during the second of the short events and in a strong wind, *Morning Cloud* carried away a winch and Owen Parker was injured, the resulting pain not helping his performance. On the Saturday came the main event, the race around the Fastnet. The wind conditions were somewhat variable, shifting between a fair breeze and spots of calm; and on the homeward run there was a pretty heavy sea running and a good weight of wind. *Morning Cloud*, with her big spinnaker set, needed two men on the helm. She used a tiller instead of a wheel, and it was Mr Heath's expressed opinion that a 40-ft boat was perhaps the largest steerable by tiller.

Trouble came when the spinnaker spars were wrenched from their tracks. The damage could not be made good at sea and defeat now seemed certain; yet the crew did manage to effect a sort of jury-rig of the spinnaker and were able eventually to hoist it, though the working of it was slow in the extreme and adjustment was virtually impossible. But off Plymouth, *Morning Cloud* was given good news by pressmen: *Koomooloo*, an Australian boat belonging to Dennis O'Neill, Kaufman-designed, had carried away her rudder, and *Cervantes II* looked like a winner. Finally, with *Prospect of Whitby* entering Plymouth ahead of *Morning Cloud*, Britain's team was in with a total of 825 points and good leads over both the Australians and the Americans; the Admiral's Cup was safe.

The third *Morning Cloud*, built to compete in the 1973 Admiral's Cup and launched in April of that year, was rather bigger than the first two, with a 45-ft overall length, the cockpit extended and with a re-arrangement of the deck gear. She fought a disappointing race in the difficult conditions resulting from a lack of wind. Eventually the Germans won, although in the latter part of Cowes Week *Morning Cloud* did well and for the first time came in to win the trophy of the New York Yacht Club; she then sailed from Cowes to win the Goodwins race from Ramsgate to the Thames estuary and round the Goodwins for home – some 50 miles. After Burnham Week, which followed, *Morning Cloud* was scheduled for return to Cowes under a fully experienced crew whose job it was to handle her when out of racing routine. As *Morning Cloud* came on passage round the Royal Sovereign lightship, a wind of 50 knots struck her, blowing across a tremendous sea. With little canvas on her, she made only very slow speed over the bottom and when not far off the Owers Light she was hit by a vast weight of water and put on her side, losing one man who was only recovered with difficulty on his lifeline, while another man was lost altogether as a result of his line parting. The yacht went about to carry out a search but he could not be found. Then another

OPPOSITE, ABOVE Edward Heath's *Morning Cloud II* in the Admiral's Cup series of 1971, narrowly avoiding collision with *Levantades*.

OPPOSITE, BELOW A tragic ending: *Morning Cloud III* wrecked on passage from Burnham to Cowes in 1973. Here she is being lifted from the sea at Shoreham in Sussex.

LEFT Prince Philip's *Bloodhound*, formerly owned by Sir Myles Wyatt, in the Fastnet race of 1959.

BELOW The German *Saudade*, Admiral's Cup winner in 1973.

crew-member – Edward Heath's godson Christopher Chadd – was lost after *Morning Cloud* was once again laid on her side.

By this time damage had occurred to the deck ribs and the vessel was taking water badly. By supreme seamanship the only remaining life-raft was got away, with two men badly hurt. Their flares were not seen and it was another eight hours before the survivors were cast up through the pounding surf on the Sussex coast near Brighton. No fault lay with the gallant crew: the south-westerly gale was said to have been one of the worst Channel blows for many years and *Morning Cloud III* had been laid low by the smashing action of heavy waves.

In 1973 the Germans swept back into ocean racing in a big way. They challenged with *Saudade* (47-ft overall) which went into the lead early on in the trials for the Fastnet, Holland, Italy, Australia, France and Britain being the runners-up. In the first of the inshore races *Saudade* came in to win six minutes ahead of the next. Two more Germans – *Rubin* and *Carina* – came in tenth and thirteenth respectively. In the next race *Saudade* was again the winner on corrected time though ninth over the line, beating *Morning Cloud* by three minutes. Subsequently, in the Fastnet, the Germans took seventh place with *Saudade* and tenth and eleventh with *Rubin* and *Carina* which gave them enough points to take the Admiral's Cup – although Brazil's entry *Saga* won the Fastnet Challenge Cup itself.

6 Round-the-World and Ocean-Going Races

*I*n 1968 came the first of the round-the-world races – *The Sunday Times* Singlehanded Race, non-stop, with a prize of £5,000; the contestants could start from anywhere in Britain, the only proviso being that the start must be made before 31 October. Out of nine contestants only Robin Knox-Johnston of the Royal Naval Sailing Association completed the course in the first race, but it was this event that led on to the Whitbread round-the-world races for fully crewed yachts. In *The Sunday Times* race, disaster had hit Nigel Tetley in his trimaran *Victress*, designed by Arthur Piver: when only some 1,000 miles off Plymouth on the homeward run, and after 27,000 miles of lone sailing, *Victress* lost her port bow and rapidly sank. Tetley, picked up by the Italian tanker *Pampero* after many hours in a life-raft, had been the first man around Cape Horn in a multihull boat, the first to take a trimaran around the world, and had made the fastest time of any yacht to circumnavigate the world, having in fact crossed his outward track some days before his boat sank. The first of the four-leg Whitbread Trophy races was held in 1973, with 16 entries. This is not an annual event, and the next race was not held until 1977 when there were 15 entries. The course was one of no less than 27,000 miles and included the notorious Cape Horn, which had not been rounded by so many vessels so close together since the great windjammers had surged across the seas.

The 1977 race was started from Portsmouth by the firing of a cannon from Southsea Castle. Competitors included *Adventure* (17·77 tons, 39 ft 2 in on the waterline), skippered by different skippers on different legs, *ADC Accutrac* (25·6 tons, 47 ft on the waterline); *Gauloises II* from France under Eric Loizeau, *King's Legend* from the Aldeburgh (Suffolk) Yacht Club, *Great Britain II* from the Royal Southern Yacht Club and the French sloop *33 Export*. Also from Britain was *Heath's Condor*. Other entries included yachts from Switzerland, Holland, Italy, the EEC and two more from France. In total 158 men and 10 women took part as crew members, coming from many countries besides those of the flags they wore.

The day of the start in September was a wet one; but the departure was watched by huge crowds from the Southsea beaches and hundreds of small craft followed them out to the starting line in the Solent. The

Trinity House vessel *Patricia* acted as a platform for the race committee to check the first stages of the race. Well away at the start were *Great Britain II* skippered by Robert James, the yacht in which Chay Blyth – still her owner – had taken sixth place in the first round-the-world race; and the Dutch *Flyer*, a 65-ft ketch under Cornelius van Rietschoten. However, these two were soon passed by *Heath's Condor*, whose name had no connexion with the former Prime Minister but was due to the sudden windfall of £20,000 in sponsorship from the Lloyd's firm of C. E. Heath, upon which her name was changed from plain *Condor*. After her came *Neptune*, a French sloop painted dark blue; next the ketch *Gauloises II*, formerly known as *Pen Duick III*, then schooner rigged; after her was the French ketch *Japy-Hermes* skippered by Jean Michel Viant, followed by *Disque d'Or* from the Swiss Ocean Racing Club, and the British *Debenhams*, another ketch of a modified Bowman 57 class, and then *Traite de Rome*, a sloop entered by the Common Market. Tenth came *33 Export*, with *Adventure*, a cutter manned by the British armed forces, close behind. Next was *King's Legend*, a Swan 65 class, followed by another of the same class, *ADC Accutrac* under Clare Francis, who in 1976 in the Single-Handed Transatlantic Race had achieved the best crossing time ever recorded by a woman. Last came the Dutch ketch *Tielsa* under Dirk Nauta, a Merchant Navy man, sponsored by Tielsa kitchenware. *Heath's Condor*, holding her lead, flew away towards the Bembridge Ledge, the only mark between the start and Cape Town. Behind *Heath's Condor* round the buoy came *King's Legend* and *Great Britain II*, just ahead of the rest.

Sailing down through the Bay of Biscay with the wind cutting in from the Atlantic is no mean test of seamanship and guts. The contestants had fair weather in the Channel but soon the wind was to blow strongly and some of the yachts faced difficulties: *Heath's Condor* had trouble with her spinnaker, while *ADC Accutrac* lost a couple of spinnakers, the first, a light triradial, even before the blow began. The Bay of Biscay was in fact kind in one sense, less kind in another: the winds fell away from time to time and progress was slow as tacking became necessary, while *Adventure* had to go in close to the shore off Cape Finisterre to try to find any wind at all. In the calms, none of the yachts making many miles, there was further trouble in the form of radio problems – *Heath's Condor* had to pick up a new set by helicopter between Tenerife and Las Palmas – and time was sacrificed over a lost forestay rigging screw in *33 Export*; this delay was to cost the French yacht quite dearly later on.

Once southward from the Canaries the racers entered the north-east trades that came steadily enough for all sail to be hoisted – but then came the Doldrums. By this time *Heath's Condor* was thought to be some 200 miles in the lead, although this was not in fact accurate as *King's Legend* at this stage was only around 18 miles behind, if to the west.

The Doldrums do not improve tempers: it is a sultry zone and often very wet, and there is no knowing from which point of the compass the wind may come if it comes at all. In the windjammer days it was commonplace for a ship to spend up to three weeks in a flat calm, her crew whistling and praying for a wind to carry them on for the Horn or the Cape of

RIGHT Eric Tabarly (left) and Chay Blyth in Portsmouth before the round-the-world Whitbread Trophy Race of 1973.

BELOW Cannon fire from Southsea Castle announcing the start of the 1977 Whitbread Trophy Race.

Good Hope. Sail has to be handled constantly in attempts to catch the smallest puff and use it to advantage. All the yachts had different experiences during this Doldrums passage, some losing many miles and much time, others finding a wind fairly quickly.

As *Heath's Condor* ran down towards the south-east trades she met trouble: the mast broke clean between the truck and the upper spreaders, the broken part falling to leeward and breaking again atop the lower spreaders. As the mast went over the side, it holed the hull and left the vessel with nothing to counteract a heavy roll. However, within a couple of hours a jury-rig had been set up and the halyards re-rove; then the crew, under Leslie Williams, set about the long business of effectively re-masting the boat. It was planned to make proper repairs in Cape Town, but in the meantime Robin Knox-Johnston, master-minding back in England, was making ready a new mast and rigging and this was flown out to Monrovia in Liberia. All this cost *Heath's Condor* seven days' delay. During this time, *Japy-Hermes* had had to alter for Recife in Brazil to seek medical attention for Patrick Therond who was suffering from a stone in the kidney.

By 22 September *Flyer* and *King's Legend* seemed to be the leaders; and at 2030 hours on 27 September the two yachts came together. However, there were still another 1,000 miles to go before they reached Cape Town. Around midnight on 4 October the Green Point lighthouse was brought up and *Flyer* came in the winner of the first leg, 12 miles in the lead of *King's Legend*.

On 25 October the race continued after four weeks in Cape Town, starting from the Fairway buoy at 1330 hours. The wind was light and southerly as the racers headed for the passage of the Roaring Forties en route for Auckland, New Zealand.

Captain Tom Woodfield, who had commanded three Antarctic research vessels and was now navigator of *Debenhams*, advised that the yachts should drop down to 55°S, thus avoiding the worst seas off shallows such as the Agulhas Bank. Ice might be encountered but this was not considered to be a very great risk.

King's Legend took the lead, with *Flyer* 40 miles west by noon next day. Calm was followed by a succession of gales to urge them along for the High South latitudes where the westerly wind never ceases to blow around the globe. Once again there were sail and rigging losses and *Gauloises II* lost her rudder early on and had to return to Cape Town under emergency steering; but she rejoined the race almost immediately. Meanwhile *Heath's Condor* was going well and soon she moved into the lead, managing to hold it right through to Auckland, taking a Great Circle track down to 55°S, as advised by Captain Woodfield – advice that not all the yachts had taken. This was a tough part of the course: the cold was intense and the wind continuous and high; some of the yachts passed glaciers on Desolation Island with the temperature dropping to −7 °F. Driving rain blew into the men's faces and added to their already soaked clothing, finding its way beneath the best that could be provided in the way of weather gear. Often this rain brought the visibility down dangerously.

RIGHT *Adventure*, a combined services entry, taking part in the 1977 round-the-world race.

BELOW *Great Britain II*, skippered by Robert James, well away at the start of the race.

Another hazard, met by *Adventure* off the Crozet Islands, was snow and sleet that froze the lips of the watchkeepers.

On 5 November *Heath's Condor* was leading *King's Legend* by 150 miles: now she ran into the same snow that had just faced *Adventure*, plus gales to propel it. Radio reports indicated pack-ice in 60 °S, reaching in places as far north as 57 °S. This report was re-broadcast by *Adventure*, and *Debenhams* (which was skippered by John Ridgeway, who had his wife aboard) turned easterly to avoid the ice; but as the wind increased up the scale to Force 10 ice began to coat her rigging. Aboard *Great Britain II* the cold was so intense that the heater's gas refused to vaporize.

Debenhams found ice on 11 November; the danger of holing the hull was extreme but skilled helmsmanship and a slice of luck kept them in the clear. *King's Legend* found a leak aft, the hull opening and closing as the rudder was worked. *Heath's Condor* lost a man overboard, but miraculously he was retrieved – his safety harness had not been clipped on, and a lifebuoy had to be thrown. There were a number of other accidents: aboard *Great Britain II* Nick Dunlop was caught by a rope and injured, nearly losing his life; this incident also resulted in the loss of a spinnaker.

King's Legend, Flyer and *Heath's Condor* now came up a little northerly towards Cape North and on 17 November *Heath's Condor* found herself some 400 miles off Hobart in Tasmania, heading up into the Tasman Sea; in the meantime *King's Legend* had moved up ahead of *Flyer* once more and on 25 November raised Cape Reinga in Tasmania with *Flyer* following three hours after. With *Flyer* in a personal race now against *King's Legend*, *Heath's Condor* entered Rangitoto Channel in the midst of a mass of spectator boats and headed for the finish, crossing the line at 0933 hours. Early next morning *Great Britain II* came in; *King's Legend* entered 75 minutes ahead of *Flyer*; *33 Export* was next in, and was declared the winner on handicap.

Given a specially warm reception later was *Gauloises II*, who was still at sea when the winners entered. She had had a very rough spin; her lost-rudder delay earlier had put her into a different weather pattern and she met continual gales. She had twice been keeled over and filled with water in tremendous seas although she had sail up. At one stage she had met 60-knot winds for a full 24 hours.

At 1100 hours on 26 December the leg to Cape Horn out of Auckland began, started by the New Zealand Prime Minister firing the gun from North Hill. The weather was fair, the spectators and their boats legion. There was an easterly breeze as the race made across Harauki Gulf, joined now by *Pen Duick VI* belonging to Eric Tabarly (an inclusion that had led to a protest by *Heath's Condor* in Auckland over the uranium content of *Pen Duick's* keel, with the result that the boat would be allowed to enter only provisionally pending a check on the validity of her rating certificate). Next morning they all took their departures from East Cape for the Horn, 4,270 miles ahead. Soon they sailed into a Force 10 gale and *ADC Accutrac* blew her jib top. Aboard *Heath's Condor* pumping became urgent as water was shipped over the side. By now *Great Britain II* was well into the lead but at the height of the gale she broke her mainsail track.

King's Legend parted a strand in a lower shroud; *33 Export* suffered badly, almost turning turtle on the first day of the New Year – 1978. Below, there was chaos everywhere, with all the gear scattered and broken. It appeared she had been taken by a solid wave which, instead of breaking, had simply seized the vessel and laid her over. Almost all the contestants suffered varying degrees of trouble and difficulty as well as the hardships of cold and wet; in the midst of all this, radio reports announced that after due consideration by the proper authorities *Pen Duick VI*'s rating certificate was invalid and she was therefore disqualified from the race – sad news indeed for Eric Tabarly.

The first of the ice was observed on 7 January by *Great Britain II*, still in the lead and around 100 miles ahead of *Heath's Condor*. It was fairly light now throughout the 'dark hours' and many icebergs were seen, though luckily not encountered. *Pen Duick VI*, still racing though disqualified, began to catch up with *Great Britain II*, while *Neptune* was doing some very fast sailing; so was *Disque d'Or*, with *Gauloises II* behind her. On 10 January *ADC Accutrac* met heavy weather and sailed close past a huge iceberg, its length estimated at a mile, with immense seas breaking over its top. The wind increased to Force 11 and the seas became vast. Next day *Great Britain II* was overtaken by the gale farther to the east and had some tough sailing to do. *Heath's Condor* was similarly engaged against the weather.

Coming up to the Diego Ramirez rocks south-west of Cape Horn, *Pen Duick VI* was leading and at 1800 hours on 15 January she passed Cape Horn, being then 21 days from Auckland. Next day *Great Britain II* came round the Cape, closing to within three miles and sailing on into another Force 10 gale. *Flyer* was now well behind as was *Heath's Condor* farther to the south. *Flyer* rounded the Horn at 1600 hours on 16 January, passing close in, with *Heath's Condor* 12 miles behind. Astern of the leaders, the remainder of the crews came past within a day of one another and *ADC Accutrac* recorded that Cape Horn was saluted with a 6-cork broadside from the champagne bottles. Two hours behind her, *Gauloises II* was caught by a huge sea that almost threw her, as the navy has it, arse over tip – but she survived after nearly diving under and broaching-to half under water. *King's Legend* was now behind *Gauloises II* and behind her again lay *33 Export*.

At last, after leaving Cape Horn, it became sunnier and warmer, but there was in fact some considerable distance yet to go before the yachts were out of the northern limit of icebergs at that time of year; and the gales were still around. Indeed, there was considerable trouble ahead: *Great Britain II* was struck by lightning, Enrique Zukveta at the wheel was thrown violently to the deck, and the compass was thrown off balance. On 24 January *Adventure* was heading up for Rio de Janeiro (the end of the third leg from Auckland) when she ran into a 60-knot storm that raged for four hours, the incredibly steep seas running up to an estimated 45 feet. The mainsail split, the helmsman was thrown clear of the wheel, and there was a shambles below, while the cockpit was completely filled with water. *33 Export* was similarly hit; one of the crew broke his leg and was later landed at Rio Grande. Before then, however, a doctor helping

ABOVE Aboard *ADC Accutrac*.

RIGHT *ADC Accutrac*, skippered by Clare Francis.

BELOW Eric Tabarly's *Pen Duick VI*, sadly disqualified because of the uranium content in her keel.

to crew France's *Japy-Hermes*, which was closing *33 Export*, had dived into a dangerous swell to bring his medical expertise to bear – an act of bravery which led to the Shipwrecked Mariners' Society presenting the trophy for outstanding seamanship to *Japy-Hermes*, a trophy well earned by the excellent navigation shown by her crew in the rescue.

Great Britain II sailed across the finish line at Rio de Janeiro just ahead of *Heath's Condor*. *Gauloises II*, who came in at 0324 hours, was the winner of the leg on handicap, with *Heath's Condor* well down the list.

The final leg for Portsmouth started at 1400 hours on 22 February, with *Great Britain II* leading from the line into a light southerly wind. By 2 March *Heath's Condor* had taken a lead with *Great Britain II* and *Pen Duick VI* a little behind. In the Doldrums *Great Britain II* lost time repairing a ripped mainsail and *Heath's Condor* increased her lead.

By 14 March most of the yachts were through the Doldrums – and also the trade winds, as the race came up into a high off the Azores. Owing to the wide extent of the high, the contestants became somewhat bunched, but soon the westerlies spread them out once more. On 20 March *Heath's Condor* believed herself quite nicely ahead of her closest rivals, and next day she was spotted by an RAF aircraft less than 300 miles off the Cornish coast. The race was to end with a tough fight against gale conditions in the Channel, by which time *Heath's Condor* was having trouble with her steering box in heavy seas. But in the early hours of 22 March the light on Portland Bill came into view, and soon after the Needles were sighted the wind dropped.

With *Pen Duick VI* some three hours behind her, *Heath's Condor* went over the line and entered Portsmouth Dockyard. *Great Britain II* came in shortly after midnight with the best elapsed or actual time (handicap disregarded) of 134 days. Two days later the Swiss *Disque d'Or* finished, ahead on handicap of both *Heath's Condor* and *Pen Duick* after a fine overall performance by her crew. *King's Legend* and *Flyer* came in later that day, the latter almost coming to grief at the last as a squall sent her broadside for Southsea beach; but she got out of her difficulties and entered ahead of *King's Legend* by an hour.

The winner on handicap of the fourth and last leg was *Gauloises II* with the Common Market's sloop *Traite de Rome* second and *Disque d'Or* third. But the overall victory and the Whitbread Trophy were *Flyer*'s, a well-deserved win for Cornelius van Rietschoten who had entered privately and without any sponsorship. Second, and the winner of the Royal Naval and Royal Albert Yacht Club Trophy, was *King's Legend*; and third, winner of the Royal Thames Yacht Club's Velsheda Trophy, was *Traite de Rome*. *Great Britain II*, the winner on elapsed time, won the Portsmouth City Council Trophy and the Royal Naval sailing Association's Gold Dolphin. These were the main prizes. There were others, among them the trophy won by *Japy-Hermes* for outstanding seamanship, and the Brownson Jewellery Trophy won by *Gauloises II* on her second leg for the most outstanding passage.

Held in alternate years, the Bermuda Race is run from Newport, Rhode Island, and today scores treble points for the winner in the Onion Patch series, started in 1964 and sponsored by the New York Yacht Club in concert with the Royal Bermuda Yacht Club, the Seawanhaka Corinthian Yacht Club and the Ida Lewis Yacht Club of Newport.

The Bermuda Race itself – the name originated from the finishing mark for the last race in the series – is the oldest of all the ocean races and was first run in 1906, its object being to encourage small boat owners to face the deep sea, following the pioneer efforts of Thomas Fleming Day who edited *Rudder*, the boating magazine of America: Day blazed the trail by taking his 25-ft boat on an Atlantic crossing with great success. From very small beginnings – only three entries in the first race, Frank Maier's *Tamerlane* being the winner – the Bermuda grew; it was not held between 1914 and 1922, but in the following year 22 boats took part, including a Bermuda-rigged yacht owned by Robert N. Bavier Senior when all other entrants still sported gaff-mainsails.

In 1932 there were no less than 43 starters, including crews from Germany, Holland and Sweden, and during this race the 78-ft American schooner *Adriane* was burned-out at sea and lost, ten of her crew being rescued by the British cutter *Jolie Brise*, sailed by Robert Somerset. From 1924 the Bermuda was alternated annually with the Fastnet. The 1938 race was the last before the Second World War, but in 1946 the Bermuda was on again.

By 1950 times were changing fast, with new classes coming along, the big yachts yielding place to smaller boats that were less expensive to sail and crew; in that year William Moore came in the winner in his Sparkman and Stephens designed 57-ft yawl *Argyll*. In 1954 there were 77 starters; by 1958 this number had grown to more than 100. In 1956 Mrs Rachel Pitt-Rivers (the actress Mary Hinton) took part in the race, the only woman to do so in the capacity of skipper; in the preceding year she had entered the Fastnet race as skipper, whilst in 1954, having already enjoyed three wins – one in the Brixham–Santander race in 1952, and two in the Cowes–Dinard – she had at the age of 57 become the first woman to be made Rear-Commodore of the Royal Ocean Racing Club.

In 1958 the great racing challenger Tommy Steele took part in his *Belmore*, designed by Captain John Illingworth's firm to conform to the rating rule of the Cruising Club of America. She carried modified sloop rig, with a transom stern and aluminium mast; in this race *Belmore* took third place overall, the first two being Carleton Mitchell and Colin Ratsey in centreboarders, the winner sailing his 38-ft 8-in *Finisterre* to victory for the second time. In the 1960 race Mitchell had his third win, still in *Finisterre*; this race got off to a slow four-day passage of light air, but then ran into a 40-knot gale with heavy rain and intense cold. As the wind came up stronger the gusts were of almost hurricane force and the yachts drove into the blown spume as the crests were hurled off the Cape Horn-like waves. The Class 'A' boat *Djinn*, belonging to Henry Morgan, was laid on her side and five men went overboard – luckily still attached by their safety harnesses – while many other yachts suffered structural damage.

In that year, *Belmore* under Erroll Bruce came in second overall. She did well through the foul conditions, putting up fine performances. Later, re-rigged as a masthead sloop to conform to RORC rules, she passed into

LEFT The 73-ft *Windward Passage*. In the 1971 Transpacific Race from Los Angeles to Honolulu she made 20 knots on occasions.

BELOW *Belmore II*, winner of the Bermuda Race in 1969. She belonged to Tommy Steele before passing into Swedish hands.

Swedish ownership – Stig Koningson's – and took part in the Admiral's Cup series of 1971.

Barring the round-the-worlders the Transpacific is the world's longest race – initially from San Pedro on the US western seaboard to Hawaii, but after 1946 from Los Angeles to Honolulu, a total run of 2,225 miles. The first was in 1906, three large yachts taking part. Others followed in 1908, 1910, 1912 and, after the war, 1923 and 1925, races in which never more than four yachts took part. But by 1969 there were 72 entries. Mark Johnson's 73-footer *Windward Passage* sailed the course in a little over nine days in the 1971 race, her speedometer showing an amazing 20 knots from time to time.

The Ton Races were started in 1899 with the One Ton Cup (or *La Coupe de CVP*) presented to the *Cercle de la Voile de Paris* by the former owners of the yacht *Estoril* when the vessel was sold to Baron de Rothschild; they are divided today into Two Ton, One Ton, Three-Quarter Ton, Half-Ton and Quarter-Ton Cups. The terms do not indicate any particular dimension but a simple relativity in size. No handicap is involved, and he who finishes first, wins.

The first race took place at Meulan on the Seine, the contestants being the French *Belouga* and the British *Vectis*, the latter belonging to the Island Sailing Club of Cowes. The French yacht took the One Ton Cup, a magnificent trophy almost three feet in height made from a solid silver block. The race between France and Britain was held each year until 1903, on two occasions taking place at Cowes. By 1907 more countries were competing, and there had been a shift to the International 6-metre rule, this lasting until 1965 when yachts from eight countries competed at Le Havre under the RORC rules. Subsequently there was a further change, this time to the International Offshore Rule; and the race now involves events of 250 miles, 150 miles and three inshore courses.

New constructions and multihulls

In 1960 the 40-ft yawl *Paper Tiger* was built for ocean racing, the first to use glass fibre in her construction. Her designer was Charles Morgan, a sailmaker, the finance coming from the American yachtsman Jack Powell. She was 27 ft 9 in on the waterline, with an 11-ft 7-in beam, a draught of 4 ft 4 in, and carried 765 sq ft of sail. *Paper Tiger* entered the Miami-Nassau Race of 1961, finishing first, ahead of the much larger *Ticonderoga* and *Ondine*. She went on to win the Southern Circuit in 1961 and 1962 before passing to a new owner, Homer Denius, in the following year.

The increasing use of glass fibre in yacht construction led to more and more offshore racing events. The Southern Ocean Racing Conference had originated with the race from Miami to Fort Lauderdale in 1928, the 1930 St Petersburg (Florida) to Havana, and the 1934 Miami-Nassau; by 1941 the Southern Circuit had come into being. In the 1960s the United States really took off with many new races: Miami to Montego Bay, Nassau to

Kingston, St Petersburg to Isla Mujeres, Fort Lauderdale to Charleston, Annapolis to Newport, Marblehead to Halifax, Sandy Hook to the Chesapeake and numerous others, among them the South Californian Newport Beach to Ensenada in Mexico which attracts more than 500 entries, a world record for a single race.

The Crystal Trophy is the multihulls' great annual race, held by the Royal Yachting Association assisted by the local clubs. Run from Cowes to Cherbourg and back around the Wolf Rock to Plymouth, it covers 311 miles. The first race took place in 1967 and was won by *Tomahawk*. In 1968 the 42-ft trimaran *Trifle* designed by Derek Kelsall set up a course record by her time of one day, 17 hours, six minutes, averaging 7·57 knots.

The Multihull Transpac Offshore Race is held biennially, from Los Angeles to Honolulu, 2,225 miles, a record being set up in 1974 by the Cabrillo Beach Yacht Club's entry *Sea Bird*. This catamaran averaged 10·53 knots to complete in under nine days, a speed of 28 knots having been recorded at one moment in the race.

For catamarans specifically there is the International Catamaran Challenge known as the Little America's Cup, which was first held in Long Island Sound in 1961. The British entry, the glass fibre *Hellcat*, owned by John Fisk and designed by Rod Macalpine Downie, was challenged by the Chapman Sands Sailing Club's *Wildcat*, which lost four of the five events. Britain held the trophy consistently until 1969 when it went to Denmark, Gert Frederiksen and Leif Wagner winning in the Thames with their *Opus III*. In the following year it was won by the Australian boat *Quest III*.

Multihulls did not appear in any numbers till about 1950, though a trimaran, the 43-ft *Ananda*, had sailed in 1946 from Cape Verde to Martinique skippered by her builder, Andre Sadrin, with a crew of two; a few catamarans (in the modern sense) had been around since 1898, when G. Herrick Duggan, a Canadian, challenged for the Seawanhaka Cup in the 36-ft *Dominion* which he had designed and built.

Since those early days multihull design, much influenced by the 70-ft trimaran *Pen Duick IV*, has rocketted in the hands of such designers as Rod Macalpine Downie, Derek Kelsall, Terry Compton, Robin Musters, Chris Hammond, Tom Lack, the Prouts, Andrew Simpson, James Wharram and John Westell. America's Dick Newick, Norman Cross, Rudy Choy, Ed Horstmann and Lock Crowther have also produced some very advanced multihulls; Crowther for instance designed *Spirit of America*, a trimaran with a 2,400 sq ft sail area. Multihulls are here to stay, and more and more of them are to be seen on the world's waterways as they increase in popularity.

OPPOSITE The catamaran *Tomahawk* won the Crystal Trophy for multihulls in 1967 – the first of these events – run from Cowes to Cherbourg and back.

OPPOSITE, INSET The trimaran *Great Britain IV* in the Round Britain Race.

7 Round-the-World Sailors and their Yachts

*T*here was beginning to be scope for the small-boat man by about the seventh decade of the nineteenth century. Those who were not rich, or concerned with the social aspects of yachting, or not over-interested in racing as such, began to be seen around the shores of Britain: one such was E. F. Knight, who took to the seas in an ex-P. & O. lifeboat of 29 ft, decked and ketch-rigged. In this boat, *Falcon*, Knight made voyages in all kinds of weather to the Scandinavian shores and found her an excellent seaboat, steering easily and taking rollers well.

R. T. MacMullen piloted his 2-ton *Leo* through Channel gales with confidence and in safety, pioneering the concept of the small boat against heavy seas and showing what could be done. MacMullen was indeed the forerunner of the lone sailor, and a number began to appear: Alfred Johnson, a fisherman from the Newfoundland Banks, took his gaff-cutter-rigged, 20-ft dory *Sentennial* alone across the Atlantic, nursing her through more than one gale and even surviving turning turtle, to make his arrival at Abercastle in Pembrokeshire after 64 days on passage. Captain Thomas Crapo crossed the Atlantic ten years after Johnson, in the *New Bedford*, a yacht of 19 ft to *Sentennial*'s 20 ft; eventually Crapo was lost while trying to make Cuba from Newport, Rhode Island, in a dory of only nine ft.

In 1894 a Finn, Captain Rudolph Frietsch, took his 40-ft schooner *Nina* from New York to Queenstown alone in 35 days. The great Captain Joshua Slocum sailed round the world alone, in the *Spray* in 1898, the first man to do so. He met many storms: off Patagonia a freak wave, a vast surge of the sea, raced for him, roaring, according to his account, as it came. He took off all *Spray*'s sail and climbed as high as possible in the rigging, and as the huge crest towered above him and submerged the 36-ft boat, he lost all sight of her decks for a while. Slocum took three years and two months to do his 46,000 miles. In 1942 Vito Dumas from the Argentine took a 42-ft ketch around the world alone in 13 months. In 1945/6 Hans de Meiss-Teuffen, a Swiss, sailed his Bermuda-rigged *Speranza* to Lisbon and ultimately to Fisher's Island, USA, crossing the Atlantic from Casablanca alone in 58 days; and Edward Allcard took his yacht *Temptress* from Gibraltar to New York in 1949 in 80 days of single-handed sailing. In 1952 Mrs Ann Davison became the first woman to sail across the Atlantic alone, in the 23-ft *Felicity Ann*, leaving Plymouth on 18 May for Dominica. With calls at Douarnenez, Vigo, Casablanca and Las Palmas, she reached the West Indies 65 days out from home.

Sir Francis Chichester

In more recent times there have been the round-the-world voyages of Chichester in *Gipsy Moth IV*, and Alec Rose in *Lively Lady*, their lonely passages via Cape Horn beginning in 1966 and 1967 respectively. Sir Francis Chichester, who took his 54-ft ketch around the world alone at the age of 65, was the first man to make the circumnavigation with only one port of call, and his was the fastest lone voyage ever made by a single-hull yacht on the west-east passage. His was also the first voyage to have commercial sponsorship, being much helped by the International Wool Secretariat. Remarkably, he had no apparent bent towards yachting until he was over 50, although he had been a first-class air pilot in his younger days and was a good enough navigator to become an instructor during the Second World War. Flying indeed was his first love and the famous *Gipsy Moths* were all named after the light aircraft in which, in 1931, he had flown alone from London to Sydney via Tripoli, then from Sydney to Japan with *Gipsy Moth* fitted as a seaplane, coming to grief in Katsura. Chichester had not been informed by the Japanese authorities that half a mile of telephone wires were running from the hill behind the town; flying right into these, he crashed and sustained 13 broken bones and a number of cuts.

The first sea-going *Gipsy Moth* was sloop-rigged, but Chichester altered her to cutter rig and refitted her to carry a five-man crew for ocean racing. Becoming a member of the Royal Ocean Racing Club, his first race was from Harwich to Rotterdam in the North Sea Race: he came in well behind the rest. However, in the next year, 1955, he won the Southsea to Harwich race accompanied by Colonel Marston Tickell, and this victory spurred him on to enter the sport in a big way. And this he did, although he was already a sick man: in that year he entered the Fastnet in *Gipsy Moth II*, doing fairly well, but was so battered by the seas that he was forced to a sickbed afterwards. However, by 1957 he was back on the racing scene and soon he was planning *Gipsy Moth III*, to be designed by Robert Clark.

This yacht was built for Chichester at Arklow in the Irish Republic, and during the building he had to face the appalling diagnosis of lung cancer, a disaster overcome by his wife's determination that there would be no operation. He came through this illness and returned to yacht racing, navigating first for David Boyer in his 11-ton *Pym* in the Cowes to Dinard Race of 1959, and navigating again in the Italian *Mait II* in Cowes Week, the races including the Fastnet. In September 1959, Chichester took delivery of *Gipsy Moth III* and the following year entered the *Observer* Singlehanded Transatlantic Race from Plymouth to New York, sailing in to a resounding win. In 1962, again in *Gipsy Moth III*, now redesigned by John Illingworth, Chichester crossed the Atlantic solo, from Plymouth to New York, fighting a long gale to bring his yacht in seven days earlier than on his 1960 crossing.

After this, and yet another Singlehanded Transatlantic race in 1964 – one that he didn't win – Chichester brooded, not for the first time, on a solo voyage around the world. Ordinary yachting did not appeal to him: his nature was such that he demanded the big challenge, and logically the last big challenge left was the circumnavigation of the globe, taking the terrible route around Cape Horn.

The famous *Gipsy Moth IV* now began to take shape in Chichester's mind; and on John Illingworth's and Angus Primrose's drawing boards she began to take life. Her builders were Camper and Nicholson of Gosport. Chichester paid weekly visits to their yard, insisting on this and that alteration and improvement, in particular Colonel Hasler's self-steering gear; this was in opposition to John Illingworth's notion of somewhat heavier gear, which he considered necessary for a boat with a high speed, as this was planned to be. Chichester was sometimes reluctant to take advice from his designers, and finally the yacht left the yard with the displacement demanded by Chichester; but in the opinion of the designers she was under-ballasted enough to make the boat tender – light and lively in the water – as it subsequently proved to be. However, as a result of the trials Chichester agreed to add an extra ton of lead ballast. Immense trouble had been taken over the design and construction, and the excellence of all this was proved in the way the boat stood up to terrible weather conditions to complete the round-the-world voyage in such record time. Nevertheless, Chichester continued, apparently, to complain in his radio messages whilst on passage and to pick holes in everything he could find.

Gipsy Moth IV was launched in 1966, after about 15 months in the building, by which time expenses were mounting fast. Some £12,000 had yet to be found to foot the bills and this was where sponsorship entered the picture: help was offered not only by the International Wool Secretariat but the Shell Oil Company, Whitbread Breweries and a number of yacht chandlers who offered to provide various accessories.

On 27 August 1966 Chichester sailed out from Plymouth at 1100 hours to the sound of the starting gun of the Royal Western Yacht Club, to face first of all a long spell of seasickness. Off Madeira a number of squalls hit *Gipsy Moth*. Chichester was having some difficulty in getting to grips with the caprices of his new and extremely lively boat: at 54 ft overall she was a good deal bigger than any of his previous yachts and a good deal less stable, and much of her design was completely new – indeed to a large extent she had been built on guesswork; luckily it had been, as one would expect of such eminent designers, intelligent and informed guesswork. A lot had been crammed into very little space: there was a fore-cabin with a bunk, a let-down bed and a sail locker; next to this was a compartment with a wash-basin, WC and wardrobe. Aft again was the saloon with two berths, six seats and a folding table. Off the saloon was a chart table and radio telephone installation, another lavatory, an oilskin stowage and a compartment containing a sea-bunk and stowage for navigating instruments. The deckhouse was heated by an oil stove; a chair, table, cooker, sink and crockery stowage were strategically placed here. Aft of the deckhouse the steering and engine controls were in the cockpit,

OPPOSITE, ABOVE
Hundreds of small boats filled the Solent as competitors for the round-the-world Whitbread Trophy Race sailed to the starting line.

OPPOSITE, BELOW The 65-ft Dutch ketch *Flyer*, overall winner of the 1977 Whitbread Trophy.

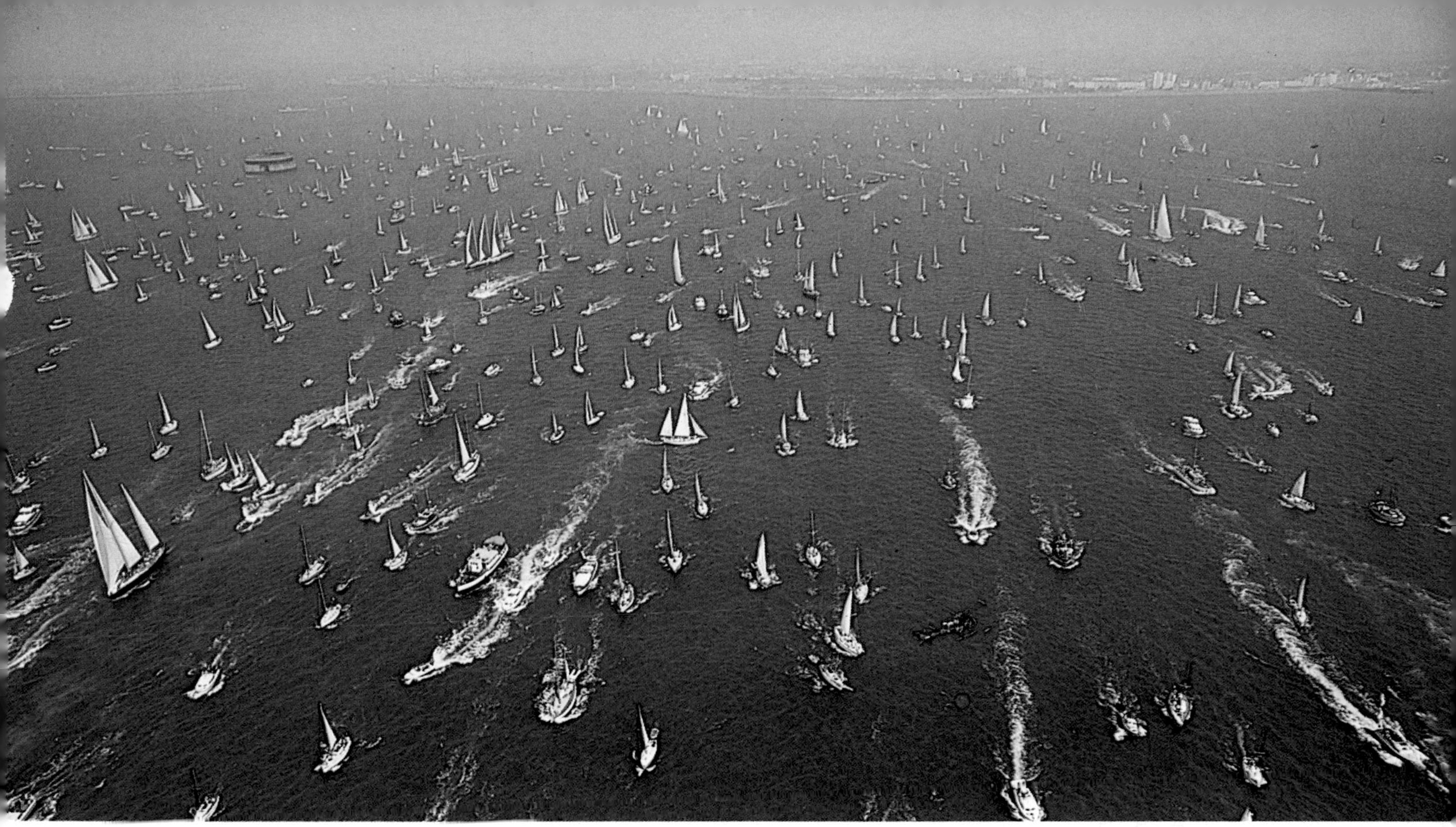

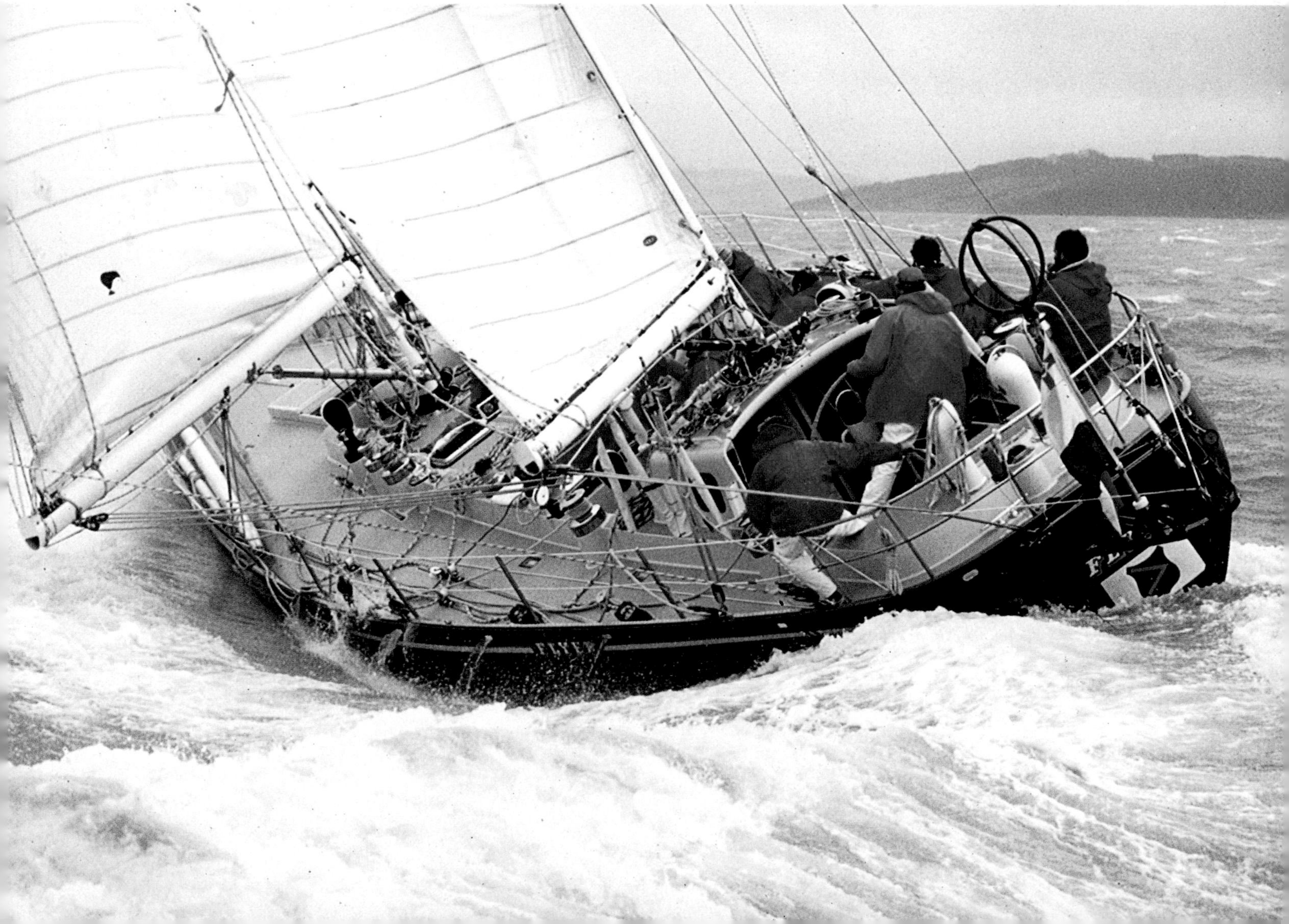
FLYER

below which were the engine and generator; a dinghy was carried aft. Below the engine compartment were the fresh water and fuel tanks. The sail area was almost 2,500 sq ft. Chichester had a tremendous amount of hard physical effort to face – the constant shifting of *Gipsy Moth*'s huge suit of sails being just a part of it. The very comprehensive stores list demanded plenty of stowage space; this was all planned to the last tiny detail by Chichester's wife Sheila, and included not only food, medical necessities and the obvious spares but also a mass of tools from nails to hacksaw blades, nuts, bolts, padlocks and chains, as well as a variety of items from coat hooks to kettles.

By mid-October he was down in the Roaring Forties, and belting along the southern seas in an easterly direction, below the Indian Ocean. *Gipsy Moth* was sailing splendidly and fast, as though she was enjoying settling down in the traces. However, things changed as the wind increased to some 55 knots, and *Gipsy Moth*'s behaviour was less than perfect in Chichester's view: at times he came close to broaching-to as he took off the sails and she laid herself across the wind; he had not expected the sudden gusts interspersed with comparative lulls and the constant changes of wind direction, and they caused him considerable difficulty. Then he had trouble with the self-steering gear, and was almost forced to abandon his hoped-for 100-day Sydney arrival; he would instead have had to make for Gage Roads outside Fremantle, Western Australia. But he managed to make repairs himself and decided after all to continue on passage for Sydney. When nearing Sydney on 7 December, to his intense surprise and irritation, *Gipsy Moth* was approached by a bunch of journalists under power, the press launch actually hitting his stern. Chichester's dismissive remarks were terse. Soon after this the yacht lost wind and three days later lay motionless in the water about 100 miles off Sydney Heads; he did not enter until 12 December, after some strenuous tacking to find and hold a wind.

In Sydney he rested as much as he was allowed to by the press, the public and the television cameras. To prepare the yacht for the Horn passage, the Royal Sydney Yacht Squadron offered docking facilities; Warwick Hood and Alan Payne, noted designers, gave Chichester their expertise in effecting alterations to the keel and the distribution of weight. A number of leaks were plugged, the sails were made good where there had been chafe and the running repair to the self-steering gear was firmed up. Whilst all this was going on, and the yacht's supplies were being replenished under the personal command of Sheila Chichester (who had arrived in Sydney aboard the P. & O. liner *Oriana*) news came through – on the night of 27 January – that Chichester had been given a knighthood. On Sunday 29 he left Sydney bound for Cape Horn.

It was a desperate run: the Tasman Sea produced one of its dreaded storms soon after Chichester had left the Heads behind. Once again suffering from seasickness as *Gipsy Moth* charged into the great breaking crests of the long seas, Chichester faced near capsize on the night of his second day out: although *Gipsy Moth*, hit by a monstrous wave, righted herself safely, the result was utter chaos, equipment being tossed around the cabin, tins

OPPOSITE *Gipsy Moth IV* on 28 May 1967 as Francis Chichester nears Plymouth at the end of his round-the-world voyage.

RIGHT Chichester's *Gipsy Moth IV* being launched from Camper and Nicholson's Gosport yard.

BELOW Francis Chichester, first man to circumnavigate the world with only one port of call.

RIGHT Chichester provisioning ship in Sydney.

of food mixing with deck equipment, and seawater pouring through the hatch. The storm kept up through the following day and Chichester admitted to a feeling of real fear for his survival. He now faced constant pumping, for the bilges were full – and not only of water: during the capsize the boards had lifted and down into the bilges had gone much of the food stocks, crockery and tools, all of which had to be fished out as time and circumstance permitted.

Covering a little more than 1,100 miles in his first seven days from Sydney, Chichester slowly closed the Horn. Just off the pitch of the Cape *Gipsy Moth* broached-to in a 40-knot gale, but came safely through. At about this time a Piper Apache flew daringly overhead, carrying men from the BBC and *The Sunday Times*. With the storm jib the only canvas aloft, Chichester triumphantly came round the Horn and into the South Atlantic; here he could head up for the Equator and more tranquil seas. On 26 March he was exactly half way between Sydney and Plymouth, and on 11 April he crossed his outward track and completed the circumnavigation. *Gipsy Moth* passed the Equator 13 days later – and was all set for the last leg of the voyage home.

Some 200 miles off Plymouth the yacht lost her wind as she had when approaching Sydney, and lay at the mercy of press boats and television launches, plus naval vessels; later the aircraft-carrier *Eagle* was in company, giving *Gipsy Moth IV* a ceremonial welcome. As Chichester approached in victory, perhaps the nicest touch of all was when a replica of his old *Gipsy Moth* aircraft flew over the little boat – nostalgic salute to a lifelong dream come true, although fulfilled by sea rather than, as he had originally hoped, by air. The eventual arrival after lying becalmed off the Lizard was bedlam: people in their hundreds of thousands cheered and waved from the Hoe and all around the Sound, the announcing gun ready from the Royal Western Yacht Club. As Chichester came past the breakwater at a little before 2100 hours on 28 May, 274 days Plymouth to Plymouth, the gun was fired and Drake's Island glowed beneath its beacon, alight, as for the Armada itself, to honour Chichester's return.

After resting and undergoing medical checks in Plymouth, Sir Francis sailed *Gipsy Moth* to Greenwich to be knighted by the Queen. Coming alongside a red-carpeted pontoon, Chichester, with his wife, walked between a guard of the Queen's Watermen in their scarlet and gold uniforms, to be dubbed by the very sword that had been used by Elizabeth I to knight Francis Drake after the circumnavigation by the *Golden Hind*.

Gipsy Moth IV never sailed seriously again, and was finally presented to the City of London by her owner, Lord Dulverton, and placed in a concrete bed at Greenwich by the Cutty Sark Society, close by the famous old clipper herself.

Sir Alec Rose

Alec Rose, a greengrocer with a shop in Osborne Road, Southsea, is close not only to the yachting scene there and across the Solent in Cowes but also to Portsmouth, the premier port of the British Navy; as an ex-RNVR himself, he loves the sea and is at home upon it. In 1964 Rose entered the

ABOVE Chichester rounds the
dreaded Cape Horn in *Gipsy
Moth IV*.

RIGHT Sir Francis Chichester,
knighted by the Queen at
Greenwich on his return from
his epic voyage. The sword
was the one used by Elizabeth
I to knight Sir Francis Drake.

Singlehanded Transatlantic Race for the first time; he came in fourth after 30 days in the attempt, and as a result of his voyage conceived the notion of making a circumnavigation.

His boat *Lively Lady* seemed unpromising: a 36-ft yawl built in 1948, thoroughly homely in appearance, though seaworthy enough as was to be proved. His original idea was to sail from England in 1966 and round the Horn before Chichester; but disaster struck in the shape of a collision soon after leaving Southsea, and Rose was forced into Plymouth for repairs, since a fair amount of damage had been done. Then, whilst in the boatyard, *Lively Lady* crashed on to her side at low water and sustained damage that would take a long time to make good. In the meantime Chichester had started on his own round-the-world voyage and Rose realized that, although he had not hoped for an actual race, he could not now achieve his original ambition.

Under his sail area of 1,853 sq ft of terylene, Rose set off again from Southsea on 16 July 1967, being given his start by the gun at the Royal Albert Yacht Club's signal station on the beach. Past the Nab Tower his escorting boats dropped away and he found himself alone – and soon in thick fog, listening to the doom-laden sound of the fog signal from St Catherine's Point on the Isle of Wight. When the fog cleared he picked up a light wind from the south, but next morning met a flat calm; this was followed by a south-westerly breeze with short seas, and he was faced with a good deal of wearisome tacking. After this came many shifts of wind and Rose made only slow progress; during the night, three days out from Southsea, he lay off Ushant with not a trace of wind to fill his sails, and in fact began to make backward progress on the adverse tide. Two nights later, however, by which time an easterly had brought *Lively Lady* to a point some 60 miles south-west of Ushant, Rose faced gale force winds and hove-to until daybreak, when he plunged on into heavy seas that broke in blinding spray over the yacht as the wind blew up harder. Then the calms came back, and it was not until the tenth day out from home that he raised Cape Finisterre at the southern extremity of the Bay of Biscay. After this the wind increased, with heavy seas sweeping down from astern, and *Lively Lady* began to press on, sometimes making 7 knots; but at the end of 13 days Rose was only 1,000 miles on his way, and thus some 300 miles behind on his reckoning. Then more irritating calms, until on the night of 2 August he sighted the Madeira Light to the south-east; soon after he picked up some better winds, moving into the North-East Trades by 6 August. That day, with a steady wind, he recorded his best run yet – 134 miles in the 24 hours, making seven knots.

Now came a good deal of rolling, the sort of movement that, if it goes on long enough, can cause wear on the deck gear. A steering rope parted, but was readily dealt with. Next day Rose covered 150 miles, driven before a Force 6 wind with gusts to Force 7, beneath a heavily overcast sky. In the next week he came past the Canaries and Cape Verde Islands, sailing fast now and beginning to make up some time. With variable winds the yacht headed on south, close-hauled. Then into the Doldrums, where Rose again met varying conditions and lost some time; when he picked up the south-westerlies he met trouble with his mainsail, which had come away from the slides on the mast. There had been chafe on the seizings and making this good was time-consuming.

Rose crossed the Equator on 26 August; though the wind was backing to the south, he could not as yet pick up the South-East Trades. He pressed on through heavy and confused seas, with constant movement that brought more strain to the deck gear; but at last came the south-easterlies. Nevertheless, by 16 September, after a harrowing time in constant gales that had proved a strain on Rose as well as on the yacht, the wind shifted to the north-west and blew up to Force 9, with huge crests rearing. So bad were the conditions then that he was forced to steer by hand; there was serious trouble with the self-steering gear – the servo-blade, or rudder, had gone. In the morning, with the wind now up to Force 10, he shipped a new servo-blade, but the foul conditions prevented him completing the repair until the following day. It was a long, hard task, but he finally achieved it successfully.

The gales continued, along with heavy rushing seas, hail and lightning, the yacht thrown about bodily day after day; they were interspersed with occasional calms but always under cloud and rain. After having to effect another running repair to the self-steering gear Rose made radio contact with Cape Town on 6 October, when he put himself some 300 miles south-west of the Cape. The next day he found a short-circuit in his radio switch-board; he was able to repair it, but until the batteries were recharged he had no current to spare for lights.

After a couple of weeks of strong gales from the north-east, the wind shifted north-westerly to bring more gales, mountainous breaking seas, and the beginnings of viciously low temperatures as Rose dropped down into the Southern Ocean and the Roaring Forties.

In the great expanses of the Southern Ocean more trouble came when the mainmast almost went overboard and he had much difficulty saving it. With his starboard lower backstay gone, he was forced to use his engine to turn and bring the wind and weather to the port side of the yacht; he was unable to complete the repair until the wind dropped next day, when he found the conditions of heavy swell unhelpful, to say the least, as he clung to the mast with hands and thighs.

Soon after this Rose suffered, as he had suffered to a lesser extent already, from severe lumbago and for three days was in such pain that he could scarcely leave his bunk. As soon as this had cleared up there was more repair and maintenance to be done, for the gear and rigging were showing many signs of wear. There were more gales, more nail-biting moments, as well as fits of depression and anxiety before *Lively Lady* came up to Split Point Light and passed Port Phillip Heads into Melbourne on 17 December. Here Rose was met by a crowd of small boats including a TV launch. His son and daughter-in-law met him, along with the police and the inevitable Customs launches.

In Melbourne Rose enjoyed rest while *Lively Lady* went in for repairs – the renewal of rigging, the fitting of extra shrouds, bottom-scraping, anti-fouling and repainting. Whilst he was in Melbourne, Rose was given the news that he had been made a Freeman of the City of Portsmouth. On 14 January 1968 he sailed out of Melbourne for Cape Horn, escorted

RIGHT A great voyage on a shoe-string: Alec Rose aboard his *Lively Lady*.

BELOW A well-deserved welcome home: Rose is escorted into Southsea after 354 gruelling days.

in the initial stages by a large gathering of small boats; he passed Port Phillip Heads as the dark came down.

On the night of 24 January, in a Force 7 gale, Rose's jib and forestays went overboard, the steel fitting breaking at the masthead. It was impossible to make this good at sea, and he carried on with his working jib and mizzen staysail; after more troubles with the rigging he entered the harbour at Bluff in New Zealand, where a complete new fitting was brought by air from England. After five days in Bluff, *Lively Lady* continued on passage for the Horn on 6 February, heading first into fog but then quickly into a Force 8 blow. Down to 48°S, the cold grew intense: now Rose was not far off the looming icebergs. This was an area of overcast skies, rain and mist; the constant bucking of the yacht in gigantic seas caused chaos below as all moveable stores shifted. After frequent gales Rose made radio contact with the Royal Fleet Auxiliary tanker *Wave Chief* off Cape Horn; and at noon on 1 April he came round the Horn itself.

Now Rose had to face further difficulties with the self-steering gear, part of which had become distorted and was twisting around: he feared that it could not be long before the gear packed up – then he would be faced with hand steering until he reached home. But, passing through another gale to reach a period of calm and fog, he was able to make a repair – a job he needed to repeat a few days later.

By 17 April the worst of the cold had been left behind but the weather was still appalling, with gales, heavy rain and thunderstorms, all alternating with calms. On 7 May Rose crossed his outward track and completed his circumnavigation, the time taken being eight months precisely. On 14 May he was back in the Doldrums, having passed through the Trades, and, crossing the Equator on 19 May, he picked up the north-east Trades to head for the Atlantic's westerlies. By 6 June he was in the latitude of the Canaries but well west by longitude; 11 days later he was some 75 miles west of the Azores and almost on track for the Channel. There followed a period of calm until a south-westerly wind came on 21 June. More gales were yet to come but the days' runs were good and by 1 July Rose was able to contact Land's End radio station. Picking up a naval escort soon after, Rose sailed on for the Nab, being met in due course by the press boats and finally by the barge of the Commander-in-Chief, Portsmouth, with Admiral Sir John Frewen embarked. The barge led *Lively Lady* in to the finishing line off the Royal Albert Yacht Club's premises on Southsea beach, where the spectators numbered around a quarter of a million people: cheers of welcome mingled with the sound of ships' sirens and rockets being fired off from the Clarence Pier. Rose was met by the Lord Mayor of Portsmouth and driven to a great civic reception at the Guildhall. He had completed his epic voyage in 354 days; it was not a fast passage, but it had been made on slender financial resources and without any form of sponsorship whatsoever and Alec Rose, soon to be knighted, had every reason to be pleased and proud. A modest man, he made little if any show of what he had done, though his achievement had been a big one: the only man to take a boat of less than 40 ft right round the world alone with only two ports of call, one of them being an emergency call for repairs. He was a much-loved hero, especially in Southsea; and his name still stands proudly above the little shop in Osborne Road.

Robin Knox-Johnston

Robin Knox-Johnston took *Suhaili* round the world in 1968/9, west to east, the first sailor to circumnavigate the globe without any port of call until Chay Blyth sailed the other way round in 1970. *Suhaili*, a 32-ft ketch, was an old-style vessel, basically a family cruiser built in India when Knox-Johnston was serving there with the British India Steamship Company and intended sailing home with some of his brother officers. He was a master mariner, First Officer of the liner *Kenya* and a lieutenant in the RNR, thus he was an experienced seaman though not necessarily in sail. He was determined that, after the efforts of Chichester and Rose, the first non-stop voyage must also be a British achievement, and he wanted to be the one to do it.

Knox-Johnston had intended selling *Suhaili* – an Arabic word for the south-east wind in the Persian Gulf – once back in England, to finance a new boat for his world voyage; but being unable to raise sufficient money, he decided to use her for the voyage and found backing from Cassell's and William Morrow, his publishers-to-be, and from the *Sunday Mirror* and *True* magazine.

Suhaili was equipped with a 38-h.p. diesel engine and her sails comprised two jibs, a staysail, main and mizzen, plus a spinnaker, all these having been flown out to Bombay by the English firm of Jeckells of Wroxham. Knox-Johnston now had her refitted by Souter's yard at Cowes and equipped with a comparatively simple form of self-steering gear devised by himself.

Suhaili left Falmouth on Friday 14 June 1968 in the Golden Trophy Race sponsored by *The Sunday Times*. The first leg was fairly humdrum: only 1,200 miles covered in the first 16 days through the Horse Latitudes and the North-East Trades, during which time he suffered from leaky bilges and was forced to do a twice-daily stint at the pump – eventually the leaks growing so bad that he was obliged to risk the sharks by going over the side to try and caulk the seams. This was only the start of trouble that was to follow him almost all the way round the world. Next came various difficulties with his sails and rigging gear, trouble with the batteries that charged his radio link – he was without radio contact for much of the voyage – and worst of all, perhaps, damage to the self-steering gear. After coping with all this, and after meeting strong gales in the South-East Trades, he came round the Cape of Good Hope and into the Southern Ocean on 3 September.

At first he met fair weather, but the barometer began to fall early on and soon the wind was blowing at gale force, accompanied from time to time by hail which made work on deck highly unpleasant. During this blow *Suhaili* was hit by a massive wave while Knox-Johnston was sleeping below, which caused more damage to the self-steering gear. The cabin was in a turmoil: apart from the horrible mess, the prognosis was bad;

ABOVE Robin Knox-Johnston's parents and Gus, the dog, watch his departure from Falmouth on 14 June 1968.

ABOVE RIGHT Knox-Johnston waves farewell from *Suhaili*.

RIGHT *Suhaili* on 18 April 1969 during her non-stop round-the-world race.

the hatch-coaming had developed leaks and there were signs that the interior bulkheads had shifted. There was a possibility that the whole roof of the cabin could go, leaving a gaping hole – a horrifying predicament signalling total disaster. However, skill and luck prevailed and Knox-Johnston sailed on to meet one gale after another in almost unbroken succession; at one stage he faced five separate gales in ten days. The damage to the self-steering gear was serious; the repair, or patch-up, took three days hard labour. In the process Knox-Johnston found that his fresh-water supply had become contaminated with bilge water. He had just enough left in polythene containers to continue, and though he considered the advisability of returning to Cape Town, he made the decision to go on, eking out his remaining water with beer and tinned fruit juice, distilling sea-water in a kettle and catching rain in a bucket.

A day or two after this unnerving discovery, he began repairs on the spinnaker, which had split down one side; whilst using his teeth to help in tying a knot, he managed to secure his moustache to the sail. Pinned down, his knife out of reach, much gritting of teeth and sharp and painful pulls were necessary before he could free himself. Later, checking the strength of his batteries with a hydrometer, he got some battery acid in one eye. Luckily his medical box yielded up antiseptic drops, the *Ship Captain's Medical Guide* provided advice, and with the eye bandaged he was able to carry on with no ill effects; but the battery charger had been swamped by a big wave and had to be dried out.

Mishaps followed thick and fast: a broken fitting caused the collapse of the main boom; in filthy weather, the worst he had seen, the boat was laid abeam to wind and sea and began to fill from what seemed like endless leaks. He considered launching his life-raft and trying to make Australia in it – but staggered on after bringing *Suhaili* back into wind and sea by trailing a line astern, after which he began sealing the leaks as best he could and manning the pump. Then came more diabolical trouble with the self-steering gear, one of its rudders breaking whilst in the heavy seas of the Great Australian Bight.

On 25 October Knox-Johnston made contact with the Australian ship *Kooringa* and by 7 November, into warmer weather by now, he was off Melbourne. Here he was able to contact a pilot boat and off-load his mail for home. He was much tempted to take *Suhaili* with all her scars and weather-weariness into port, but resisting this he carried on towards the north-eastern tip of Tasmania and then on for New Zealand towards Cape Horn. There followed a period of fair weather, but soon more trouble came when *Suhaili* was taken aback by a suddenly freshening wind: the tiller broke clean off at the rudder head as Knox-Johnston pushed it hard over to right the boat. More time had to be spent on makeshift repairs, and with a shortened tiller *Suhaili* sailed on.

In the early morning of 17 January 1969 he picked up the Diego Ramirez rocks, and by evening the Horn was in sight eight miles or so to the north-east. Six days later the yacht was off Port Stanley in the Falklands, after which more gales were met before she ran into calms; on 3 February, after four-and-a-half months of the Southern Ocean and its roaring winds and air of dead depression, *Suhaili* came up into the South Atlantic proper.

RIGHT As *British Steel* leaves Southampton Water Chay Blyth faces the prospect of a single-handed passage round Cape Horn from east to west, against the prevailing winds.

BELOW Hard work aboard *British Steel*, an unremitting element of such a marathon voyage.

Soon he had picked up the South-East Trades and in 12 more days was across the Equator.

At 1135 hours on 21 April he raised the Bishop Rock Light; and at 1525 on Tuesday 22 *Suhaili* entered Falmouth, escorted by HMS *Warsash*, the Falmouth lifeboat and the tug *St Mawes*, to a rapturous reception by huge crowds of spectators – the winner of the long race in 312 days, and indeed the only one of the nine entries to finish the course.

Knox-Johnston was later awarded the CBE in recognition of an amazing feat of endurance and a remarkable capacity to take seemingly insuperable difficulties in his stride. He had had plenty to overcome. He had suffered much from the appalling loneliness and boredom that occur when there is nothing that actually cries out to be done; he speaks of the psychological effect of crossing the 40th South Parallel, into an area where foul weather is always to be expected as an inescapable fact of life. Anxiety and doubt are enemies also; fear of possible illness striking when far from shelter; fear of damage to sails and gear in the endless storms – damage that it might be beyond one's capacity to put right; moods that swing between the extremes of black depression and a possibly dangerous optimism that can border on euphoria; worry about families at home when radio contacts are lost for long periods; and the just as painful worry about *their* worrying when no letters or reports can be sent out.

In Knox-Johnson's case the answer to periods of mental vacuum, consuming anxiety or fits of deep depression was to fill his thoughts with something creative, such as writing poetry or reading; and it is interesting that he speaks – and he is not alone in this – of the power of God as an undoubted force which gives a man support in meeting the dangers and hardships of a long and lonely voyage. 'God's almighty hand' becomes, far out at sea, a very living thing.

Chay Blyth

A Scot and former paratrooper, who in 1966 had rowed in an open boat across the Atlantic with Captain John Ridgeway of the Parachute Regiment, Chay Blyth's claim to fame rests largely upon his extraordinary feat in taking *British Steel* singlehanded around the world the other way – from east to west, right into the very teeth of the dreaded westerlies blowing off Cape Horn. From port to port – Hamble to Hamble – Blyth took 292 days, in the course of which he made the longest windward passage ever completed by a yacht.

Why did he attempt the apparently impossible? No-one had ever done it singlehanded before: that was reason enough for Chay Blyth. Knox-Johnston, Chichester and Rose had done it the other way; now there was nothing else left to do.

British Steel, built by Philip and Son of Dartmouth, designed by Robert Clark and sponsored by the British Steel Corporation, was a ketch of 59 ft overall, with a beam of nearly 13 ft; her full load displacement was 17 tons and she carried a big sail area of around 1,500 sq ft. Blyth took *British Steel* out of the Hamble River on Sunday 18 October 1970 to sail south for Cape Horn. After much tacking in the early stages, with head winds from the start, he came up against a number of minor snags: a sheared pin in the self-steering gear, a speedometer defunct after hitting a floating piece of timber, and other annoyances. On the second night out he spoke to his wife Maureen on his radio telephone; this he found an unsettling experience, for his mind filled with thoughts of all the tasks she was faced with alone after his departure. For her there must have been a kind of anti-climax in his sailing, apart from the prospect of many months of anxiety: it had been Maureen who had, among many other things, overseen the vital storing of *British Steel* and who had personally varnished all the hundreds of tins of food, hard labour but something that has to be done when tins are taken aboard a small boat and need to last a long while.

On the fourth day out, a running-pole – used to spread out the headsails – broke, and there was too much wind and sea for Blyth to make a repair immediately. Later there was a rendezvous off Madeira for exchanging mail and handing over such film as he had taken for television purposes. After this Blyth found fair weather, but during this period the second running-pole broke when a sudden gust took the boat one night when Blyth was sleeping. He made a repair, but the pole went once more before he met the Doldrums; these brought not the expected calm but a succession of squalls with rain and lightning when he had either to take off sail or run headlong before the wind.

On 14 November he crossed the Equator, some 28 days out from home. Into the trades, he set a course westerly towards the coast of Brazil. He began to pick up shipping, sighted two large whales – and then struck some ferocious thunderstorms, some of them right overhead. As he came off the Argentine coast he met the *pampero*, the sudden heavy gusts that come tearing off the pampas: one after the other they came, the wind gusting up to 55 knots. During one of these viciously sudden squalls the mainsail jammed, which meant that until he could clear the sail it would be impossible to take it off if another such squall should come. Later a *pampero* struck him at 60 knots, and *British Steel* was laid over, but righted as Blyth brought her round.

By now, as he dropped south for the Horn passage, the weather was growing extremely cold; on Monday 21 December he raised the peaks of Staten Island off Tierra del Fuego, around 150 miles north-east of the Horn itself. The weather pattern had made Blyth decide to sail round Staten Island rather than attempt the Le Maire Strait lying between Staten Island and the mainland of Tierra del Fuego.

He met very confused seas, and again a number of whales. Two days later, after sailing through comparative calms, he was closing Cape Horn; he made his planned rendezvous with HMS *Endurance* and had his first human contact for many weeks; he took over stores and passed back his mail and films. On 24 December he rounded Cape Horn, and on Christmas Day, already feeling deprived of family and proper celebrations, he met dirty weather, the wind howling at Force 8 to 9. Huge seas swept the ketch, while overhead the spume blown off the tops of the Cape Horn greybeards formed a continuous curtain of water. One of the huge rollers damaged the self-steering gear beyond his capacity to repair; and Blyth himself was

OPPOSITE With its sturdy Bermudian ketch rig, *British Steel* was the strongest and the most carefully devised of all the single-handers.

flung across the cockpit and badly cut on the forehead. Now, with the self-steering gear out of action, he was forced to heave-to whenever he needed rest; as a result, he found himself being blown south towards the dangerous pack-ice of the Antarctic seas. Fortunately, after a period of serious danger, a shift of wind took him back on to his right course for the Pacific Ocean.

By this time Blyth had found that his equipment was wearing out because of constant use; the cold was getting worse and his heating stove had packed up beyond repair; he was tacking constantly to the shifting winds and he was tired almost to the point of exhaustion. He suffered badly from chilblains, and callouses appeared on his hands from constant manning of the ropes. It was a miserable experience, and Blyth confesses to many feelings of loneliness and homesickness and a desire to be able to stretch his legs and walk on shore, away from the boat's confines. He even had to force himself to cook. On 2 January 1971, after he had passed through some moderate weather, the real blows came in again from the south-west, winds that rose to Force 11; *British Steel* lay with bare masts at the whim of wind and sea, and when after two days the gale eased Blyth's sights showed him that he had been blown some 200 miles north.

After this he met four days of fairly thick fog, during which he grew more and more depressed and uneasy. This was succeeded by long swells with little wind, and the ketch rolled badly, but soon afterwards he found a good wind that sent him north-westerly at around eight knots. By now he was having to contend with a number of leaks; not all were traceable, which led to his having to lie in a constantly wet sleeping bag.

On 1 February he sighted land, the first since Cape Horn five weeks earlier; this was an island south-east of New Zealand. Eight days later he crossed the International Date Line – half way round the world now, a great occasion for a lonely man, now homeward-bound. As he came towards New Zealand there was another (unscheduled) rendezvous, this time with a TV crew; on succeeding days he met calms and made some contacts with fishing vessels. Then more gales blew up and during a hard southerly buster a good deal of damage was done on deck, while the cabin below was flooded by a big wave, everything bursting out from the various stowages. On 5 March he rendezvoused in Tasmania's Storm Bay and then headed away clear for the Cape of Good Hope, still battling straight into the teeth of the westerlies. Here he sailed into what he considered to be the worst part of his voyage. The start from Tasmania was made in calms and light winds, though with immensely long rollers sometimes up to 30 ft high that came in succession to sweep below the ketch and lift her up – only to be zoomed down into the water-valley on the other side. During the night of 7 March the weather worsened sharply and, though it occasionally improved thereafter, squalls and heavy seas lay in wait ahead, seas that dropped aboard and did much damage above and below. At one stage the mizzen sail was ripped almost to pieces, the cabin was flooded again and the pump became inoperable; when a calm came there was a vast amount of maintenance and repair work to be done by a weary man. Then came the real gale-force winds, the spindrift blown off the tops of the gigantic waves as though Blyth were still below Cape Horn. On the night

OPPOSITE Robin Knox-Johnston surrounded by a carefully planned stock of provisions as he prepares at Plymouth for his solo non-stop voyage.

of 8 May, when beginning to approach the Cape of Good Hope, he was almost run down by a large vessel – later he found she was Russian – and only deflected her by letting off one of the explosive charges he had brought to scare away whales.

Shortly after this Blyth was firmly in the shipping lanes and, with his self-steering gear still out of action, had to remain at the tiller right through the night hours. On 22 May he rendezvoused off Cape Town with a South African naval vessel and soon after this he turned up towards the South Atlantic, sailed through some more bad weather initially, then came into the southerlies and a more comfortable ride. On 10 June he passed St Helena and seven days later was in radio contact with Portishead, the first British station for many months. On the 22nd he crossed the Equator once more, and on 28 July made contact with HMS *Ark Royal*, whose sailors cheered ship as they passed him. Friday 6 August saw Chay Blyth back in the Hamble River where he was met by Prime Minister Heath and members of the royal family, including the Duke of Edinburgh.

Like Chichester, Rose and Knox-Johnston, Chay Blyth had undergone terrible physical dangers and exposures; but he too found that loneliness was much the most dangerous enemy, and one that leads to depression and sometimes to despair. Blyth emphasizes that radio contact is of immense importance in lifting depression: the human contact that comes through the disembodied voices of family and friends. He also speaks of the heartening effect of knowing that so many people, watching his progress worldwide via the radio reports, and helping him by keeping in touch, were with him in spirit as he battled on through the stormy seas at the bottom of the world.

Another round-the-worlder who speaks of depression is the French Alain Colas who sailed the Chichester route around Cape Horn in 1974 in his trimaran *Manureva*, completing the course in 57 days less than *Gipsy Moth IV*, calling only at Sydney. Colas almost came to grief at the start when a gas leak only just failed to extinguish him while he was sleeping; but it was not this that depressed him. Depression, curiously, came from a comparatively fair-weather rounding of Cape Horn; possibly it is the case that the Horn's desolation gets to the bone deeper and faster when there is not enough to do to divert the mind. Colas established a record in his passage to the Azores from the Equator: he took 13 days, his speed on this leg being not far short of that of the great *Cutty Sark*'s best.

In 1977/8 a woman, Naomi James, sailed alone around the world, backed by Quentin Waller and by Chay Blyth who supplied the boat; and once again Chay's wife Maureen was at the tin-varnishing. Naomi James left on the west-east passage on 9 September 1977, and after the usual storms and vicissitudes, and after suffering the breakdown of radio contact in the South Atlantic, she returned in the summer of the following year to be made a DBE.

Nourishment is of the highest importance on voyages such as these; something to sustain the body through all kinds of weather, hot and cold, storm and calm. The lone sailors mention the beneficial effects of whisky – Sir

OPPOSITE *Suhaili*, very small and isolated on a vast expanse of ocean. Built entirely of teak to traditional boatbuilding methods, she proved to be well balanced and withstood her marathon superbly.

LEFT AND BELOW On 9 June 1978 thousands turned out at Dartmouth to welcome home Naomi James, who beat the record with a solo round-the-world voyage of 272 days in her 53-ft yacht *Express Crusader*.

Alec Rose took a little each morning with his cup of tea – and though none of them made undue use of it, its presence brought comfort. Among the essential items were sugar, porridge, cereals, potatoes, including instant mashed, biscuits, tinned or packeted soups, baked beans, butter, tinned or powdered milk, and eggs and bread for as long as they lasted. Fruit was important, as were fruit juices. Tinned beer was often welcome. The tinned stock would also comprise sardines, herrings in tomato sauce, meats, corned beef, rice pudding, sausages. Cocoa, Ovaltine and tea bags were usually included; and Rose took Complan, that instant standby to give energy and food value.

They all, of course, had cooking stoves; Rose preferring calor gas. He always, when possible, had a substantial breakfast: cereal or porridge, fried eggs with potatoes and onions followed by fruit. Lunch was usually tinned meat of one sort or another, with vegetables and baked beans. His supper was a light meal of cheese and biscuits with butter and perhaps a slice of cake – and he liked his nightly cocoa. There was a need to plan one's diet and to impose a strict discipline in the preparing of proper meals: no skimping to save the bother. After all, a man's body *is* his food, and the fitness of the body was vital.

What next? It has all been done now: round the world alone west to east; with two ports of call; with one port of call; with no stops at all. Round the world the other way; round the world by a lone woman. Now it remains either for someone to circumnavigate backwards, or to set age as the criteria: the first child under six, the first man over a hundred, then the first geriatric woman? It seems to be all that is left. But nothing can take the glory from those few – still very few – who tried and succeeded.

Acknowledgments

Photographs were supplied or are reproduced by kind permission of the following:

Associated Press 65 above, 102 below

Beken of Cowes 8, 17 below right, 48 above, 51 below, *54*, 56 above and below, 58 above and below, 63 below, 69 below, 71, 78 above and below, 81 above, 83 above left, above right, below left and below right, 85 above and below, 95 below, 106 below, 112 above, 115 below, 118 above and below, 121 below.

Bettman Archive 21 above right and below, 67 below

Alastair Black 98–9, *125* below

Camera Press 75 above and below, 92 above right, 104 below, 110 above, 112 below, 115 above left and above right, 121 above, 128 below, 136 below

J. Allan Cash 92 below (photo Eileen Ramsay), 95 above left (photo Eileen Ramsay), 97, *100*, 106 above (photo Eileen Ramsay), 128 above left and above right (photos Eileen Ramsay)

Mary Evans Picture Library 15 below, 17 above, 32 below, 38 below right, 45 above, 48 below right, *53*

Photo by courtesy of the Rt Hon. Edward Heath 104 below

Illustrated London News 110 below, *125* above

Keystone Press 146 above and below

Mansell Collection 15 above, 30 below left, *35*, 41 above and below, 63 above, 65 below, 88 below

National Maritime Museum 12 above and below

Popperfoto 67 above, 69 above, 92 above left, 95 above right, 102 above. 133 above, 138 above

Radio Times Hulton Picture Library 17 below left, 19 above, 22 above left, 32 above, 38 above and below left, 45 below, 48 below left, 51 above left, 60 above, below left and below right, 81 below, 88 above

Royal Library, Windsor (copyright reserved) 28 below, 30 above

Royal Thames Yacht Club 26–7 (photo Eileen Tweedy)

Royal Yacht Squadron, Cowes 25, 28 above, 72 (photos Photographic Records Ltd)

Syndication International 126, 130 below, 133 below, 136 above left and above right, 138 below, *141*, *143*, *144*

Topix 130 above

Weidenfeld and Nicolson Archives 19 below, 51 above right

Page numbers in italics refer to colour illustrations

Picture research by Deborah Pownall

The author wishes to acknowledge in particular and with much gratitude the willing help given to him by the staff of both the reference section and the lending section of Worthing Central Library in the procuring of a large number of books for research.

Bibliography

Andrews, Allen, *The Whisky Barons*, Jupiter Books, 1977

Antrobus, Paul; Ross, Bob; Hammond, Geoffrey, *Ocean Racing Around the World*, Angus and Robertson, 1975

Blyth, Chay, *The Impossible Voyage*, Hodder, 1971

Bradford, Ernle, *Three Centuries of Sailing*, Country Life, 1964

Brassey, Mrs, *Voyage in the Sunbeam*, Longmans, Green, 1878

Bruce, Erroll, *Cape Horn to Port*, Nautical Pub. Co., 1978

Chamber's Encyclopedia

Chichester, Francis, *Gipsy Moth Circles the World*, Hodder, 1967

Crabtree, Reginald, *The Luxury Yachts from Steam to Diesel*, David and Charles, 1973

— *Royal Yachts of Europe from the 17th to the 20th Century*, David and Charles, 1975

Dear, Ian, *Enterprize to Endeavour, The J-Class Yachts*, Ian Allan, 1977

Dodgson Bowman, W., *Yachting and Yachtsmen*, Geoffrey Bles

Duff, David, *Victoria Travels, Journeys of Queen Victoria between 1830 and 1900 with Extracts from her Journal*, Frederick Muller, 1970

Gavin, RN, Paym.-Cdr. C. M. *Royal Yachts*, Rich and Cowan, 1932 (limited edition)

Heath, Edward, *Sailing – A Course of my Life*, Sidgwick and Jackson, 1975

Heaton, Peter, *Yachting History*, Batsford, 1955
The Singlehanders, Michael Joseph, 1976

Heckstall-Smith, Anthony, *Sacred Cowes*, Allan Wingate, 1955

Hoyt, Edwin P., *The Vanderbilts and their Fortunes*, Frederick Muller, 1963

Fea, Allan, *The Flight of the King*, Methuen, 1897

Follett, Tom; Newick, Dick; Morris, Jim, *Project Cheers*, Adlard Coles, 1969

Francis, Clare, *Come Wind or Weather, ADC Accutrac Races Round the World*, Pelham Books, 1978

Frischauer, Willie, *Onassis*, Bodley Head, 1968

Johnson, Peter, *The Guinness Book of Yachting Facts and Figures*, Guinness Superlatives Ltd, 1975

Knox-Johnston, Robin, *A World of my Own*, Cassell, 1969

Illingworth, Capt. John H., *The Malham Story*, Nautical Pub. Co., 1972; *Twenty Challenges for the America's Cup*, Hollis and Carter, 1968

Kavaler, Lucy, *The Astors*, Harrap, 1966

Kürenberg, Joachim von, *The Kaiser, a Life of Wilhelm II, Last Emperor of Germany*, trans. H. T. Russell and Herta Hagen, Cassell, 1954

Leather, John, *World Warships in Review 1860–1906*, MacDonald and Jane's, 1976

Leslie, Anita, *Francis Chichester*, Hutchinson/Hodder, 1975

Lewis, David, *Ice Bird*, Collins, 1975

Lilly, Doris, *Those Fabulous Greeks: Onassis, Niarchos and Livanos; Three of the World's Richest Men*, W. H. Allen, 1971

Martin, Ralph G., *The Woman He Loved: the Story of the Duke and Duchess of Windsor*, W. H. Allen, 1974

Massie, Robert K., *Nicholas and Alexandra: an Intimate Account of the Last of the Romanovs and the Fall of Imperial Russia*, Gollancz, 1972

Nicholson, John, *Great Years in Yachting*, Nautical Pub. Co., 1970

Page, Frank, *Solo to America, The Observer Single-Handed Race, 1972*, Adlard Coles, 1972

Phillips-Birt, D., *Yachting World Handbook*, Iliffe Books Ltd, 1967, St Martin's Press, NY

— *The History of Yachting*, Elm Tree Books and Hamish Hamilton, 1974

Rose, Sir Alec, *My Lively Lady*, Nautical Pub. Co. with Harrap, 1968

Simper, Robert, *Victorian and Edwardian Yachting From Old Photographs*, Batsford, 1978

Slocum, Capt. Joshua, *Sailing Alone Round the World*, Rupert Hart-Davis, 1963

Tetley, Nigel, *Trimarin Solo, 'Victress' Round the World*, Nautical Pub. Co., 1970

Waugh, Alec, *The Lipton Story*, Cassell, 1951

Williams, Geoffrey, *Sir Thomas Lipton Wins*, Peter Davis, 1969

Index